PUSSY RIOT!
A PUNK PRAYER FOR FREEDOM

PUSSY RIOT!

A PUNK PRAYER FOR FREEDOM

LETTERS FROM PRISON, SONGS, POEMS, AND COURTROOM STATEMENTS,
PLUS TRIBUTES TO THE PUNK BAND THAT SHOOK THE WORLD

THE FEMINIST PRESS
AT THE CITY UNIVERSITY OF NEW YORK
NEW YORK CITY

Published in 2013 by the Feminist Press
at the City University of New York
The Graduate Center
365 Fifth Avenue, Suite 5406
New York, NY 10016

feministpress.org

Cover design by Herb Thornby
Text design by Drew Stevens

ISBN 978-1-55861-834-3
[Cataloging-in-Publication Data available upon request]

Contents

Tributes to Pussy Riot

Preface

This compilation of texts was first put published as an e-book by the Feminist Press within the month following the verdict delivered on August 17, 2012, in which three members of the feminist punk band Pussy Riot were sentenced to two years in a penal colony for felony hooliganism. The event that led to the conviction was a forty-second performance by five women in a priests-only section of Moscow's Cathedral of Christ the Savior. They call their song a punk prayer. It asks the Virgin Mary to become a feminist and "put Putin away."

In the course of their detention, Maria Alyokhina, Nadezhda Tolokonnikova, and Yekaterina Samutsevich (known as Masha, Nadya, and Katya) wrote letters, prepared court statements, and made these and their poems and songs available to a wide audience. We at the Feminist Press, along with millions of people around the world, have been reading. These declarations are stunningly articulate about the plight of civil rights in Russia, and about the corruption at the core of the government there, which is in strategic alliance with a powerful religious institution. These texts are also brilliantly expansive about broader social issues of gender equality and human rights.

There's a word that makes many people uncomfortable to say. It's often used as a euphemism for something that should be taken more seriously than it is. The euphemizing is usually a response based in fear or ignorance by people who just don't want to think about something as messy and possibly out of control in the human story. This word has been embraced by an increasingly populous subculture that wants to expand the demographics of who gets seen and heard. This appropriation of a term understood to be negative or diminutive is a sign of solidarity with those at the bottom of the world's power structure. Of course, the word I'm thinking of is *riot*. Call an uprising a riot, and you question the values of those in pursuit of change, without ever saying so. Through their performance, writings, and actions, Pussy Riot has accomplished something very important. In risking their own status as citizens, they have called into question the values and moral authority of those who have for so long abused power and dominance—what feminists have referred to as the patriarchy.

I've been thinking about why this performance stirred such harshly punitive reaction from a government that must surely now regret the attention they have bestowed upon the band. And why we outside of Russia feel such affinity with the band. Pussy Riot's punk prayer creates a challenging juxtaposition. Is it possible for a punk to pray? Can a renegade, someone who believes in insurrection, also believe in a higher power? Isn't that what prayer is—a belief that something exists beyond the visible or material world, to which or to whom we can appeal for justice or relief? I have always believed in the transformative power of music. When punk came along, it felt like the (im)perfect mix of my desire for pop music's hit of energy with a radically declarative form of expressing opposition. Opposition to what? Where to begin . . . It's the clarity and distillation of Pussy Riot's message and style of delivering that message which awes me and my colleagues at the Feminist Press and riot grrrls and rock stars and activists and journalists everywhere. Pussy

Riot's message is articulated in the texts contained in this book. It is also expressed by their status as prisoners of conscience. We have thousands of people incarcerated in the US alone, simply for their oppositional views. If Pussy Riot draws attention to the plight of the world's unjustly incarcerated populations, their contribution will be immeasurable. Prayers might even be answered.

It's exciting to imagine this: five masked women performing in a priests-only section of an Orthodox church, which has historically and systemically denied women equal rights and proselytized against homosexuality. This radical display of dissent, and the punitive response to it, has galvanized us to speak out for freedom—for Pussy Riot, and for everyone who suffers at the hands of corruption and a morally bankrupt system. Feminist Press wishes to amplify this message; we offer this book as a historical document as well as a call to action.

On October 10, 2012, Pussy Riot appealed the guilty verdict. Katya's sentence was suspended, but Nadya and Masha's appeal was denied. Freepussyriot.org is joined by other organizations taking donations for Pussy Riot's legal defense and other related expenses. Proceeds from the sale of this book will also support this fund.

Almost immediately after Masha, Nadya, and Katya were arrested, their letters and statements started to appear online in English. Many of those translations were the basis for the texts in this book. I want to thank all the translators and editors of these translations, those who we know of and list here, and all of those who have helped but whose names we do not know. With graditude: Maria Corrigan, Elena Glazov-Corrigan, Marijeta Bozovic, Maksim Hanukai, Sasha Senderovich, Liora Halperin, Katharine Holt, Vera Koshkina, Ainsley Morse, Rebecca Pyatkevich, Bela Shayevich, Keith Gessen, *Chto Delat News*,

Christian MilNeil, Gila Primak, Alisa Obraztsova, Margarita Shalina, Sarah Valdez, Angelica Sgouros, and Jeanann Pannasch. I apologize to anyone who has worked on these texts and who is not acknowledged here. Any omission is unintentional.

I would also like to acknowledge the websites, online magazines, and blogs that have published Pussy Riot texts, and continue to offer important documents, news, and updates on this case. n+1's website has been a lead source of these texts, and we thank them for continuing to enrich the literary landscape. We also could not have gotten this book together without the support of Robert Lieber, Alisa Obraztsova, Christian MilNeil, JD Samson, Yoko Ono, Johanna Fateman, Justin Vivian Bond, Eileen Myles, Karen Finley, Bianca Jagger, Tobi Vail, Barbara Browning, Peaches, Simonne Jones, Vivien Goldman, and Laurie Weeks.

When I say "we" at the Feminist Press, I mean the most dedicated and inspiring group of coworkers I could possibly imagine. We are Gloria Jacobs, Jeanann Pannasch, Drew Stevens, Maryann Jacob Macias, Cary Webb, Elizabeth Koke, Angelica Sgouros, and Amy Scholder, along with an amazing, ever-changing crew of interns.

Finally, thank you, Maria Alyokhina, Nadezhda Tolokonnikova, Yekaterina Samutsevich, and the Pussy Riot collective. You are speaking out, and we are listening. I am reminded of Karen Finley's refrain: "Life is more important than art. But life is meaningless without art." We support your courage and provocation, and encourage everyone, in their own ways, to fight the power with you.

—Amy Scholder
New York
November 2012

Virgin Mary, Put Putin Away
(Punk Prayer)

Virgin Mary, Mother of God, put Putin away
Put Putin away, put Putin away!
(End chorus)

Black robe, golden epaulettes
All parishioners crawl to bow
The phantom of liberty is in heaven
Gay pride sent to Siberia in chains

The head of the KGB, their chief saint,
Leads protesters to prison under escort
In order not to offend His Holiness
Women must give birth and love

Shit, shit, the Lord's shit!
Shit, shit, the Lord's shit!

(Chorus)
Virgin Mary, Mother of God, become a feminist
Become a feminist, become a feminist!
(End chorus)

The church's praise of rotten dictators
The cross-bearer procession of black limousines
A teacher-preacher will meet you at school
Go to class—bring him money!

Patriarch Gundyaev believes in Putin
Bitch, better believe in God instead!
The belt of the Virgin can't replace mass meetings
Mary, Mother of God, is with us in protest!

(Chorus)
Virgin Mary, Mother of God, put Putin away
Put Putin away, put Putin away!
(End chorus)

Art or Politics?

March 23, 2012

O ur performance in the Cathedral of Christ the Savior was a political gesture to address the problem of the Putin government's merger with the Russian Orthodox Church (ROC).

Patriarch Kirill has repeatedly evangelized on behalf of the political figure of Putin—clearly no saint—and continues to urge his parishioners not to participate in protest rallies. A joint political action carried out by governmental authorities and the Orthodox Church before the elections for the State Duma, the "Two Days' Wait for the Belt of the Virgin," was aimed at portraying an image of apolitical Orthodox citizens.

This outrages us no less than the violation of the elections of the Duma. Therefore, we have introduced a new element to our performance—a prayer—and called our punk public prayer "Virgin Mary, Put Putin Away." In this statement, we respond to the political activity of the faithful, and counter the Patriarch Gundyay's efforts to distort the truth.

And we needed to sing it not on the street in front of the temple, but at the altar—that is, in a place where women are strictly forbidden. The fact is, the church is promoting a very conservative worldview that does not fit into such values as freedom of choice; the formation of political, gender, or sexual identity; critical thinking; multiculturalism; or attention to contemporary culture. It seems to us that the Orthodox Church currently lacks all of these virtues.

With regard to the consequences of our performance, we were surprised by the fury and scale of the smear campaign that followed, and by the arrest of three women based on unverified reports on the Internet of their involvement. The range of threats that people have made against us is out of scale with our activism. We believe that as part of his post-election campaign, Mr. Putin, who received the so-called "victory" in these elections, has decided to avenge all the wrongs that were inflicted against him through the citizens' opposition. Most likely, this attack has been a punishment for our Red Square performance of the song "Putin Has Pissed Himself."

But it was our performance in the Cathedral of Christ the Savior that provided the formal excuse for the criminal proceedings that followed. Now the authorities are emboldened and are trying to push another charge against the suspects—the charge of extremism—because the chorus of our song "Putin Has Pissed Himself" begins with the words "Revolt in Russia." We are outraged by the fact that people thought to be involved in opposition circles are being rounded up on the street and held in custody. The girls being detained do not recognize themselves as members of our group. As far as we know, they went on a hunger strike, which lasted for twelve days.

Notes

In November 2011, a few weeks before Russia's national parliamentary election, the Russian Orthodox Church in Moscow sponsored a traveling exhibition of a famous religious relic, the Holy Belt of the Virgin. Pilgrims waited for up to two days to see the relic, and the event conveniently monopolized news coverage as growing public protests were threatening Putin and his United Russia party.

"Gundyay" is a diminutive variation of the patriarch's secular name, Vladimir Mikhailovich Gundyaev. The use of a secular nickname here is intended to bring the patriarch down a notch.

The extremism charges were ultimately not pursued. Instead, authorities charged the women with felony hooliganism and incitement of religious hatred.

The jailed women initially denied involvement in Pussy Riot; since then, they have affirmed their membership in the group and affirmed their participation in the punk prayer.

Letter by Masha in Prison

March 5, 2012

This letter was given to Masha's friends by one of her lawyers, Nikolay Polozov. It was written when she wasn't allowed to send mail. She was later transferred to a more densely populated prison cell.

Second day of pretrial detention.

My only cellmate, Nina, and I sleep on metal beds in outdoor clothes. She sleeps in a fur coat; I sleep in a coat.

It's so cold in the cell that our noses turn red and our feet are ice cold, but we are not allowed to get into bed or under the covers before the bedtime bell. The holes in the window frames are stuffed with hygiene pads and bread crumbs. The sky is orange from street lamps at night.

I've officially stopped my hunger strike so I now drink warm colored water (tea) and eat dry bread three times a day. The flat metal bed is terrifying; it seems easy to smash your head against the edges.

Nina keeps saying that it won't get any worse. She's fifty-five. She got detained for burglary. A drunken policeman took all her stuff and forced her to sign the report incriminating her; she never got to read what she signed. Now she's a thief in a mask. She's one of Pussy Riot too.

Nina told me that her cellmate before me was named Vika. She got handcuffed and raped in a police station, despite her being pregnant. She was only brought to the doctor the next day. The doctor did not diagnose the miscarriage or the rape. Vika is charged with burglary of an unidentified person, that's what the report says. She's also a thief in a mask.

And yes, she's one of Pussy Riot too.

I still can't sleep. I got threatened with being transferred to a disciplinary cell for not making up my bed properly today. Here, in the pretrial center, no one knows what a duvet case is. But everybody knows that you're a criminal and here for a "good reason."

Nina keeps saying it won't get any worse.

We talk about Orwell, Kafka, and the governmental structure. We curse injustice, but despite my encouraging quotes from Foucault, Nina doesn't believe in change. She keeps saying, "This might be it, but I won't leave."

As long as the doctor at the pretrial detention says proudly that he's been to opposition protests in Bolotnaya Square, as long as the woman in uniform who takes my fingerprints believes in the revolution (though she finds the peacefulness of it pointless)—as long as all those who write about me and who help me feel happy about these changes—I won't leave.

Today is the first day I've been able to go for a real walk. During my time out in the tiny square yard between concrete walls, with rusty metal bars on the ceiling, I ran for twenty minutes.

We are not allowed to receive any books at Pretrial Detention Number 6; the only book that's allowed is the Bible, which my mum brought to me this morning. I still haven't got it.

It seems like it really won't get any worse.

Letters by Nadya in Prison

March 29, 2012

"And take heed to yourselves, lest at any time your hearts be overcharged with surfeiting, and drunkenness, and cares of this life, and so that day come upon you unawares." —Luke 21:34

The people that I had the chance to work with during my actionist years were quite unusual for Moscow. These people were not interested in money or comfort. They did not go to the Jean-Jacques Café. When they wanted to go to a café they would choose one where they could be active in discussion, in planning actions, without having to order anything. When they wanted to eat, they would break a loaf of bread together. They preferred not to spend their time or their consciousness, with which they were ready to include and transform everything around them, on the daily grind and the struggle for creature comforts. Their hearts were not heavy from overeating or drunkenness. Their minds were fully occupied with whatever they were currently working on. They worked a lot, with fervor and enthusiasm. Even the knowledge that they might have to pay for their activities with prison did not stop them. In general, they were busy with self-education or training or taking action out of virtue. Philosophers should not merely describe the world, but change it. Happiness is to live by virtue. I am happy. Even here, sometimes.

"In your patience possess ye your souls." (Luke 21:19) I find it difficult to bear being apart from those who make up my life. But I am being patient. I am learning how to socialize with those who currently surround me. The people around me have sought to attain comfort in life. For all of them, their status in life was important. But now we are equal to one another in terms of our comfort. Most of them cannot understand how one can engage in political art without being paid for it. "I don't understand 80 percent of what you are saying," said a young girl booked for narcotics under Article 228 [of the Criminal Code of the Russian Federation], when I tried to explain to her why I participated in meetings and took part in political actions. "You've been brainwashed," "Who is paying for all of this?" "Surely you have smart men who are organizing all of this!" is what I constantly hear from those booked for narcotics under Article 228. Whereas those who are in for fraud under Article 159 do, in part, understand me, as they sympathize with [Mikhail] Khodorkovsky, [Aleksei] Kozlov, and [Olga] Romanova, but they are also convinced that we are part of a larger political scheme that involves smart men and significant funding. But I actively engage with my fellow cell mates; I explain to them the meaning and motives of my activities; and some of them in the SIZO [Investigation Detention and Isolation Center Number 6] have already come to believe that the Pussy Riot activity emerged through the power, energy, will, and aspirations of a handful of politically active young people.

Jesus Christ was accused of blasphemy. If Article 213 had existed two thousand years ago, Christ would have been charged under it. He called upon our asceticism and selfless devotion, but the tsars of the world, not wishing to do without their limousines and flashing lights, have judged him for it. "But beware of men: for they will deliver you over to the courts," Christ warned. (Matthew 10:17) Beware, but go and prophesize to them. Without a penny in return, cursed and lied to, walk the earth and prophesize both to the Jews and the Hellenes.

Two thousand years later, Pussy Riot, with its much more modest challenges (we do not seek to establish a church, we merely suggested scrutinizing some aspects of the earthly representatives of the Christian church), entered the Cathedral of Christ the Savior, and were thrown behind bars, delivered over to the courts. We are not messiahs. But who knows, maybe Pussy Riot is a sign of the new times in the spiritual history of mankind—the century of liberty, as prophesied by Russian religious philosophers. All of this past Sunday I took notes on the epistles of the apostles. I was interested in the issue of the succession of law and grace, relative to the old and new letters. It was on this contrast that [Dmitri] Merezhkovsky, [Nikolai] Berdyaev, and [Sergei] Bulgakov established their teachings concerning the future emergence of a new milestone to crown history—the era of liberty, which should arrive after the epoch of Christ's love, righteousness, and faith as proclaimed by the Old Testament. Who knows, perhaps the inclusion of human rights and liberties as priorities in the politics of the West in the twentieth century is also another sign of the approach of the era of liberty and creativity, as well as the Pussy Riot concert.

Berdyaev taught that creativity is the structural moment of the age of liberty. Love will transform itself into liberty and with it the world will change. It is already in motion.

August 16, 2012

My imprisonment does not anger me. I don't hold grudges—not personal grudges, at least. I do, however, hold political grudges. Our imprisonment is a clear sign that freedom has been taken away from us, from the entire country. This threat of destruction to Russian liberation and emancipatory forces is what makes me angry. We all must see the big picture in small events, a tendency in a constellation of seemingly random signs, and a common trend in specific occurrences. Second-wave feminists said "the personal is political." It's true. The Pussy Riot case is showing how three people who are charged with disorderly conduct can give birth to a political movement. This special case of suppression and persecution of those who dared to speak up against an authoritarian country stirred up the entire world: activists, punks, pop stars, government officials, comedians, environmentalists, feminists, Islamic theologians, and Christians. All of them pray for Pussy Riot. These private problems have become a truly political matter.

The Pussy Riot case is bringing together diverse and multi-directional forces. I still have a hard time believing that this is not a dream. The unbelievable happens in modern Russian politics: the demanding, persistent, powerful, and consistent pressure of society on government authorities. I am grateful to everyone who said, "Free Pussy Riot!" We are all making history—an important political event—and Putin's system will find it harder and harder to control us. Whatever Pussy Riot's verdict is, we are already winning. We have learned how to be politically angry and vocal.

All Pussy Riot collective members are happy that we have been able to inspire action by our fellow citizens; we are happy that your political passion is so strong that it has been able to unite people of different languages, cultures, ways of life, and economic and political status. Kant would have said he did not see any other reason for this miracle than the moral foundations of being human. Thank you for the miracle.

Death to Prison, Freedom to Protest

The joyful science of occupying squares
The will to everyone's power, without damn leaders
Direct action—the future of mankind!
LGBT, feminists, defend the nation!

Death to prison, freedom to protest!

Make the cops serve freedom,
Protests bring on good weather
Occupy the square, do a peaceful takeover
Take the guns from all the cops

Death to prison, freedom to protest!

Fill the city, all the squares and streets,
There are many in Russia, beat it,
Open all the doors, take off the epaulettes
Come taste freedom together with us

Death to prison, freedom to protest!

Letter to Patriarch Kirill

March 26, 2012

"Blessed are those who are persecuted because of righteousness, for theirs is the kingdom of heaven." —Matthew 5:10

Your Holiness, Patriarch!
A fervent and sincere prayer can never be a mockery, no matter its form. Therefore it cannot be said that we jeered at or mocked the shrine. What troubles us is that the very shrine that you consider so defiled is so inseparably linked to Putin, who, as you say, returned it to the cathedral. And this is why you perceive our prayer—asking our Holy Mother to drive out those who defile the brightest ideals of human life in Russia, and all possible precepts of the Orthodox faith—as a mockery of the sacred.

In the prayer in question, we expressed our grief—shared with millions of Christians—that you had allowed the religion to become a weapon in a dirty political campaign, that you had urged the faithful to vote for a person whose actions are far removed from God's truth. We simply cannot believe the representative of the Heavenly Father if he acts against the values for which Christ was crucified on the cross. As Pushkin said, "It is impossible to pray for King Herod; the Mother of God forbids it."

You were greatly mistaken when you stated in your sermon that we do not believe in the power of prayer. Without believing in the power of prayer, would we have prayed so desperately and fervently in the temple, even in anticipation of the severe persecution that might fall on us and our loved ones? Would we pray in the face of this repressive apparatus of earthly power, which bides its time to avenge itself against anyone who takes a stand on behalf of civil society?

The power and truth of our prayer did not shame the faithful, for surely the faith of a true believer, like the feelings of Christ, are too deep and universal—too filled with love—to be shamed. Our prayer shamed only Putin and his henchmen, and because of that, three women have been thrown in prison, taken away from their young children, and subjected to daily insults by the state's bureaucracies. It is the non-believer Putin, who, through domination and division, needs to keep the women in jail.

You say that we believe only in propaganda, the media, lies, slander, money, and weapons. But we don't have faith in any of those things that today rival even the power of King Herod, on whose behalf you called on us to vote, and to pray, and in whose name you associate the prosperity of the Russian soil.

First the pervasive and false propaganda on state television wrested a victory for Putin away from the people, and then, through outright falsehood, these same forces are trying to assure the people that women with young children should be kept in custody for "violation of the laws of the church."

On whose side are propaganda, the media, lies, and slander? On whose side is the belief in money? On which side are the performers of Pussy Riot, whose lives exhibit the asceticism necessary for creative thinking? Or does the faith in money reside with those who invested in the empty values of unprecedented government-sponsored luxuries for any high-ranking man? With those who also have faith in weapons? With those who call for murder in the name of religious feeling? Or with the men who hired the armed gang that shouted and wielded weapons during the raid on March 3, on a mission to arrest two women suspected to have been in the temple and of having asked the Virgin Mother of God, loudly, to get rid of Putin?

We believe, contrary to what you preach to the congregation, only in the power of prayer, only in the power of art, only in the power of words, and only in the power of the love of our friends and loved ones—that is the extent of our faith, and in its service we possess nothing more than our songs and our prayers. For those who threw three women in prison, and for those who demand continued repression, further arrests, and additional criminal cases, indeed, for all those entities that you associate yourselves with—for you, it's money, guns, lies, slander, the media, and propaganda. For us, there is only a burning desire to bring to our people the truth.

We will pray for those who would wish many years of prison and torture of Nadezhda, Maria, Yekaterina, and the rest of us. We do not believe, in today's world, that it is possible to remain a Christian and demand prison and savage punishments for those whose prayer sounds different or rises from a non-canonical place. We admire the humanity and tolerance of Jesus, and his ability to save and uplift people, and to this ideal we should all strive, regardless of our faith. After all, even the most hardened atheist cannot help but recognize the enormous contributions to human ethics that Christ's teachings delivered.

What would Christ say upon learning that some people, who call themselves His followers, did not object that on Forgiveness Sunday, Putin's henchmen brought a criminal case against prayer as if it were a serious crime? What would Christ say, knowing that in the sad days of Lent some Christians rejoice that three women have been detained in a terrible prison for praying?

We have explained thirty thousand times that our prayer could not be "a mockery of the most holy," because we prayed to the Virgin in defense of our sacred land. We pray that Our Lady should give courage and strength to our people to drive out King Herod and his servants, and banish them to make their lives in accordance with the human conscience.

Note

Patriarch Kirill, who has taken a vow of poverty, has repeatedly been seen wearing a $30,000 Breguet timepiece that he has long denied owning. In early April 2012, shortly after this letter was written, Kirill became the butt of jokes throughout Russia when an obviously doctored photograph appeared on the church's official website showing the Patriarch's sleeve-covered wrist above a clear reflection of the watch in the tabletop.

Kropotkin-Vodka

Occupy the city with a kitchen frying pan
Go out with a vacuum, get off on it,
Seduce battalions of police damsels
Naked cops rejoice in the new reforms

The fucking end to sexist Putinists!

Kropotkin-vodka splashes in bellies
You feel good, but those Kremlin bastards
Face the revolt of the toilets, fatal poisoning
Flashing lights won't save you, Kennedy will meet you

The fucking end to informant bosses!

Caught some ZZZs, time to oppress the day
The knuckle-duster's ready, feminism's sharpened
Take your soup to Eastern Siberia
So that the Riot will become rough enough

The fucking end to sexist Putinists!
The fucking end to sexist Putinists!
The fucking end to sexist Putinists!

Letter to President Medvedev

The following is Pussy Riot's response to Dmitri Anatolyevich Medvedev's comment that the members of the group had "achieved their goal," during a television interview the Russian President gave on April 26, 2012, to journalists from five television networks. This response was written after the president refused to consider the evident violation of the principles of the law in the Pussy Riot case.

"Freedom is when you forget the name of the tyrant."
                                                        —*Joseph Brodsky, 1975*

"Freedom is a unique feeling, which is different for each person."
                              —*Dmitri Anatolyevich Medvedev, April 26, 2012*

Dmitri Anatolyevich!
        Exactly four years ago in May 2008, a few days before your inauguration as president, members of the art group Voina ["War"] visited some police stations near Moscow to place your portrait on the wall as a newly elected president, next to the existing portrait of Putin.
        Activists from the group Voina called your inauguration day

"a great achievement of the Russian people," "a victory of freedom," and declared May 7 an important holiday—even more important than the other May holidays.

Your portrait, affixed to the prison bars of the police departments around Moscow, encapsulated the hopes of millions of Russians in 2008. Your bright image was meant to penetrate into the darkest corners of the judicial, political, and penitentiary systems of the country to confront the monstrous medieval barbarity that characterizes Russian law today.

Four years passed.

Atrocities and torture committed by your so-called police force have become increasingly systemic. [Sergei] Magnitsky, a lawyer, was executed in prison; his persecutors got a raise and were nominated for awards. [Mikhail] Khodorkovsky and [Alexander] Lebedev got another big prison term. Taisiya Osipova has been in prison already for a year and a half without any medical help; she might hope that, after your regal attention to her case, she could embrace her daughter again a year or two before her ten-year sentence is due to end.

It is touching, as you said in your interview, that you see "a lot of sense" in the fact that today, "all of these cases have become public, transparent." Over the last four years it has become absolutely transparent that in every serious situation in which conflicting interests demand legal justice, the Russian court will take the side of the stronger party, the side of those who have never bothered to pay attention to the law.

You proudly consider yourself a practicing lawyer. However, as you have repeatedly emphasized, in reality a period of four years was not long enough to carry out the reforms that would bring Russia closer to a constitutional state. It was not enough time to educate a new judiciary or police force. Four years were not enough to wean public officials from bribes and to stop them from hating their own people. Four years were not enough to develop and implement your beloved electronic systems that were supposed to make stuffing ballot boxes impossible.

Four years: this is also the age of the children of our group's imprisoned members—Gera and Filipp, the daughter and son of Nadya Tolokonnikova and Masha Alyokhina, respectively. The court that you slowly and carefully reformed during the last four years has left these children without their mothers.

What is going on in the mind of our practicing lawyer as he observes (of course you have already mentioned several times that as the head of state, you are not able to influence justice before a verdict is made) how the court of our nation first refused to detain the professional sadists—the policemen who tortured and killed people using bottles of champagne—and then twice extended the detention of women who, from the point of view of the religious institution, made a prayer in church but with the wrong intonation?

As a practicing lawyer, does it not trouble you that Yekaterina Samutsevich, one of the members of Pussy Riot, is being held in the same prison cell in Pechatniki prison where Major Yevsukov awaited trial in 2009? Is it possible to maintain your self-respect as a legal professional and accept the authority of the court when someone whose crime was a prayer in church should be isolated from society in the same conditions as a police chief who shot civilians with his service weapon?

During your television interview you responded quite cynically to Pussy Riot. You mentioned that the participants in the act had accomplished what they had hoped. Not without reason, the journalists around you presumed that you referred to the accomplishment of getting into prison. But, after a dramatic pause, you clarified your belief that we were merely seeking fame and celebrity.

We would like to assure you, Dmitri Anatolyevich, that the monstrous reaction of the Russian authorities to the punk prayer "Virgin Mary, Put Putin Away," and the widespread outrage of huge numbers of people who cannot understand why three women are in prison—these are the things that have brought about our so-called celebrity. It is not on our merit that Pussy Riot gained international attention. In the same interview, even you at the end of your reign forcefully emphasized that nothing has actually changed during the last fifty years in Russia. It was you who made the candid observation that, just as it was a half a century ago, a person of culture must resist the government, even through imprisonment and prosecution.

Naturally, many of your colleagues and subordinates—including the Ministers of Justice and Culture, and the heads of the Federation Council and of the President's Council on Civil Society Development—came out openly against the imprisonment of the members of Pussy Riot. To them it is evident that this trial will result in a public disgrace for Russian authorities. However, today the opinion of one man is more significant than all the power of collective intelligence and even your starry-eyed abstract notions of freedom. That is why our group appealed to the Virgin Mary to banish this man from Russian politics.

Thus the end of your presidential term will be remembered for the victory of bondage over freedom in Russia—the very opposite of your ambitions. The three girls imprisoned in Pechatniki in Moscow are unequivocally recognized by the international community as prisoners of conscience and serve as a vivid warning of Russia's current path.

And this path is due solely to a very specific idea of freedom: a freedom in which one person, acting alone, is allowed to make the important decisions in our country.

Putin Has Pissed Himself

A rebellious column moves toward the Kremlin,
Windows explode inside FSB offices.
Bitches piss behind the red walls
Riot calls for the system's abortion!

Attack at dawn? I am not against it,
For our joint freedom, a whip to chastise with
Madonna to her glory will learn to fight
Feminist Magdalene go demonstrate!

Revolt in Russia—the charisma of protest!
Revolt in Russia—pissed on by Putin!
Revolt in Russia—we exist!
Revolt in Russia—riot! Riot!

Take to the streets
Live on the Red
Set free the rage
Of civil anger!
(loss on the square)

Discontent with the culture of male hysteria
Wild leaderism devours brains
The Orthodox religion of a hard penis
Patients are asked to accept conformity

The regime heads toward censorship of dreams
The time has come for subversive clashing
A pack of bitches from the sexist regime
Begs forgiveness of a feminist wedge.

Revolt in Russia—the charisma of protest!
Revolt in Russia—Putin got scared!
Revolt in Russia—we exist!
Revolt in Russia—riot! Riot!

Take to the streets
Live on the Red
Set free the rage
Of civil anger!

Opening Courtroom Statement by Masha

The indictment says that I committed disorderly conduct motivated by religious hatred and enmity, and by hatred of Orthodox Christians. I fundamentally don't understand this statement. Our performance aimed to attract the attention of the Russian clergy and the rector of the Cathedral of Christ the Savior, Patriarch Kirill. We are representatives of our generation, and we are at a loss after his actions and public appeals.

We wanted and continue to want a dialogue. We know that there is no other way to get an audience with any representative of the church authority because of their security force, who, ironically, are allegedly victims in our case. We wanted to get Father Kirill's attention because we wanted to ask him about his decision to ask the people to vote for Vladimir Putin [during the presidential election of March 4, 2012]. I am an Orthodox Christian, but I hold other political views, and my question is: What should I do?

As a representative of my generation, I also have questions about the relationship of the church and the state to Father Kirill. I would sincerely like answers to these questions from Father Kirill, and rely on his wisdom. I thought that the church loved its children, but dual standards turn out to be present here as well: the church loves only those children who believe in Putin. I never thought that the Russian Orthodox Church was meant to call for faith in any president; I thought its only role was to call for faith in God.

It is important for me to understand whether the church will grow along with society or if it will remain a conservative institution. In the search for an answer, I did not expect such a repressive and inquisition-like reaction. Therefore, I consider the prosecution's claim of our criminal motive unfounded. We did not have any such motive. The rehearsal recordings show that we aimed for a minute-and-a-half performance, of which we actually performed only forty seconds. To say that our forty-second performance undermined centuries-old foundations is absurd.

Further, the prosecution argues that we intentionally bought clothes for this performance. The materials of our case directly refute this point. Tights and dresses are a part of the Pussy Riot image, and the balaclavas, identified in the indictment as "masks," are not a disguise, but a conceptual element of our image. Pussy Riot does not want the focus of attention on girls' appearances, but creates characters who express ideas.

We chose the day of our performance purposefully. It was Maslenitsa, Butter Week, with its tradition of dressing up and dancing. We came to the cathedral outside of the hours for service or other celebratory activities, which indicates that we did consider the church calendar.

The prosecution alleges that we violated the public order out of hatred and enmity of religion and hatred of Orthodox Christians. I think this is a fantasy, and I have already explained our motivation above. In no way could I have imagined the scale of the reaction that exists today. It was not me who organized broadcasts on the federal television channels where we were labeled as blasphemers and instigators. It remains unclear to me why all this has happened and continues to happen. Moreover, I think the organizers of such television programs themselves depreciate the Russian Orthodox tradition when they argue that three girls could do something to the spiritual foundation of the state, even more so with their God; this is especially true because my friends and I repeatedly tried to make peace between our supporters and those who condemn us. If religious people are offended that we climbed into the fenced pulpit and treated it like a stage, then for that I apologize. We did it because we did not know the internal church rules.

If our six-month imprisonment was required to explain these rules to us in detail, then I can confidently say we have learned and understood them.

Everything I said above is an ideological question about the indictment presented to me, the very statement of which I consider absurd because I am a citizen of a secular state. All my deeds and misdeeds, I believe, should be addressed in the legal realm. I consider our performance an administrative offense, but it was transferred to the legal realm due to the influence of administrative, political, or religious elites. I ask an independent court to conduct an independent investigation and establish the truth.

Once again, I claim that I never had any religious hatred of Orthodox Christianity.

Opening Courtroom Statement by Nadya

The punk band Pussy Riot, to which I belong, is a musical group that conducts unexpected performances in different urban spaces. Pussy Riot's songs address topical political issues. The interests of the group members are political activism, ecology, and the elimination of authoritarian tendencies in the Russian state system through the creation of a civil society.

Since its origin in October 2011, the band has played concerts in the subway, on the roof of a trolleybus, on the roof of the detention center for administrative detainees, in clothing stores, at fashion shows, and on the Lobnoye Mesto in Red Square. We believe that our art should be accessible to everyone, therefore we perform in diverse public spaces. Pussy Riot never means to show disrespect to any viewers or witnesses of our punk concerts. This was the case on the roof of the trolley bus and on the Lobnoye Mesto, and this was the case at the Cathedral of Christ the Savior.

On February 21, 2012, the Pussy Riot band performed its punk prayer "Virgin Mary, Put Putin Away," at the Cathedral of Christ the Savior. In early March 2012 three members of the group were imprisoned because of our music and political activism. The themes of our songs and performances are dictated by the present moment. We simply react to what is happening in our country, and our punk performances express the opinion of a sufficiently large number of people. In our song "Virgin Mary, Put Putin Away," we reflected the reactions of many Russian citizens to the patriarch's calls for votes for Vladimir Vladimirovich Putin during the presidential election of March 4, 2012.

We, like many of our fellow citizens, wrestle against the treachery, deceit, bribery, hypocrisy, greed, and lawlessness particular to the current authorities and rulers. This is why we were upset by the political initiative of the patriarch and could not fail to express that. The performance at the Cathedral of Christ the Savior was not committed on the grounds of religious enmity and hatred. Equally, we harbor no hatred toward Orthodox Christians. Orthodox Christianity worships the same values we do: mercy, forgiveness, justification, love, and freedom. We are not enemies of Christianity. We care about preserving the good opinion of Orthodox Christians. We want all of them to be on our side—on the side of anti-authoritarian civil society activists. That is why we went to the cathedral.

We came with what what we have: our musical performance. During this performance we intended to express our concern that the rector of the Cathedral of Christ the Savior and the head of the Russian Orthodox Church—the patriarch—supports a politician who forcefully suppresses the civil society that is dear to us.

I would like to emphasize that, while in the cathedral, we did not utter any insulting words toward the church, toward Christians, or toward God. The words we spoke and our entire punk performance aimed to express our disapproval of a specific political event: the patriarch's support of Vladimir Vladimirovich Putin, who took an authoritarian and antifeminist course of action. Our performance contained no aggression toward the audience, but only a desperate desire to change the political situation in Russia for the better. Our emotions and expressiveness came from that same desire. If our passion appeared offensive to any spectators, we are sorry for that. We had no intention of offending anyone. We hope that those who cannot understand us will forgive us. Most of all, we want people to hold no grudges against us.

We very much wish that people would not see our denial of guilt under Article 213, Part 2 of the Russian Criminal Code as audacity, insolence, or our unwillingness or inability to admit our mistakes. It seems to me that those who were distressed by our songs tend to interpret our denial of guilt in this way. I believe that we are all victims of the most perfect misunderstanding and confusion of words and legal terms.

My key point is that I separate the legal and ethical assessments of our performance of "Virgin Mary, Put Putin Away." This is a very important—probably the most important—thing in this proceeding. I insist that the criminal side of our story must not be confused with the ethical one. Our denial of guilt does not mean our unwillingness to explain our actions or to apologize for the distress brought about by our performance, and I would like everyone, especially the victims, to try to understand that.

My assessment of the Pussy Riot punk prayer is this: our ethical mistake was that we brought our newly developed genre—the unexpected political punk performance—to the cathedral. We did not think that our actions might offend some. In fact, we have performed in various places throughout Moscow since October 2011, and everywhere—in the subway, in stores, on the roof of the detention center, on the Lobnoye Mesto—people received our actions with humor, cheerfulness, or, at the very least, with a sense of irony. Similarly, based on the experience of our previous performances, we had no idea that our punk performance could hurt or offend someone. If anyone was offended by our performance at the Cathedral of Christ the Savior, then I am ready to admit that we made an ethical mistake. This was, indeed, a mistake because we had no conscious intent to offend anyone. Our ethical—I emphasize ethical and not criminal—fault lies in the fact that we allowed ourselves to respond to the patriarch's call to vote for Vladimir Putin with our performance at the cathedral, to share our political position on his political statements with an audience. This is our ethical lapse of judgment, and I emphasize and acknowledge it, and I apologize for it.

However, our ethical slip matches no article of the Criminal Code.

We have been in prison for five months now, but our actions do not constitute a crime. Our violation of the rules of church conduct differs substantially from the accusations that we now face, of hatred and enmity toward the entire Orthodox religion and all its believers. One does not follow logically from the other. I shudder every time I read the indictment that we went to the cathedral out of contempt and hatred toward Christians. These are terrible, awful words and incredibly strong, terrible accusations. Our motivation was purely political and artistic. I agree that, perhaps, we did not have an ethical right to bring them into the cathedral's ritual space. But we do not hate anyone.

Think about it: What are hatred and enmity? Neither is a joke. No one should label people with them just like that. Perjury is happening here. For five months we have suffered from slander. It is not easy for me to withstand being cynically and cruelly labeled with feelings that I have never experienced toward any living being on earth. The prosecution accuses us of hiding our true motives (which supposedly are religious hatred and enmity) to avoid punishment. However, we do not lie; we have principles, and one is to always tell the truth. We did not betray our principles even though the investigators detained us and tried to force us to admit our guilt under Article 231 (Part 2). Such an admittance would label us with false motives—hatred and enmity—and crush and destroy us as honest people. The investigators repeatedly told us that if we plead guilty, we would be released. We refused.

If we admit our guilt under Article 231 (Part 2), we defame ourselves. The truth is more precious to us than anything, even more than our freedom. Thus, I think there is no reason not to trust our words. We will not lie, certainly. The content of our laptops and hard drives is presented in the criminal case, and it refutes the prosecution's version of our motives. These materials prove that we were not motivated by religious hatred or enmity. Anyone who considers the content of our laptops and hard drives will clearly see that our motivation was purely political. Volumes 3 and 4 of our criminal case contain our criticism of Putin's authoritarian policies and our reflections on the benefits of peaceful civil protests. Volumes 3 and 4 contain our texts about feminism and interviews with the Pussy Riot band. Not a single word is about religious hatred or enmity.

In all of those laptops and hard drives, the prosecution has not found a single piece of evidence confirming this suggested motive, and now they are trying to get out of their predicament by making illogical conclusions. In our interviews after our performance on February 21, 2012, we repeatedly said that we treated Christianity with great consideration and respect. The prosecution, realizing their lack of evidence of our religious hatred, has resorted to the next move. They now claim that our statements of loyalty toward Christianity were meant to cover up our true attitude toward the religion in an attempt to minimize the backlash against the illegal act we committed at the cathedral. These statements are illogical because we have publicly stated our positive attitude toward religion on February 21, 2012, and on other dates—way before the news that a criminal case had been initiated against us.

The conclusion that we "seek revenge for Hypatia's death" is so absurd that even people who still doubted our intentions now realize that the prosecution has absolutely no evidence of the motive of hatred. Therefore neither the motive nor the elements of a crime exist.

Two expert reports ordered by the investigation found no motive of hatred or enmity in our actions. However, for some unfortunate reason, the indictment fails to mention these reports. The experts concluded that none of our song lyrics, our activities, or our video contain any linguistic features of dishonor or insult toward Orthodox Christians, the Orthodox church officials, or other religious groups. Neither do they contain any linguistic evidence of hostile attitudes toward the Orthodox religion, Orthodox believers, or people of other religious groups. Moreover, the experts noted that the behavior of our group had no psychological signs of hostility: the girls did not commit aggressive or violent acts against anyone.

In summary, we had no motive of religious hatred or enmity, nor did we conduct any crime under Article 213, Part 2 of the Criminal Code of the Russian Federation.

Note

Hypatia of Alexandria, an ancient Greek philosopher in Roman Egypt, was the first historically noted woman in mathematics. She taught philosophy and astronomy in Alexandria at the time when positions in science were predominantly occupied by men. Hypatia was highly regarded for her knowledge, extraordinary dignity, and virtue. She died in an incident when Christian monks seized her on the street, beat her, and dragged her body to a church, where they mutilated her flesh and burned her remains.

Raze the Pavement

Egyptian air is good for the lungs
Do a Tahrir on the Red Square
Spend a violent day among strong women
Look for scrap on the balcony, raze the pavement!

It is never too late to become a dominatrix
The bludgeons are loaded, the screaming gets louder,
Stretch the muscles of your arms and legs
The cop is licking you between the legs

The toilets are clean, the chickens are in their civvies,
Specters of Zizek washed away in the toilets
Khimki Forest plundered, Chirikova banned from elections,
And the feminists sent home on maternity leave.

Excerpts from the Court Transcript

DAY 1

*Candle seller Lubov Sokologorskaya takes the stand first. She tells
the court that she tried to follow the women as they headed for
the altar but was stopped in her tracks by God. This was when the
women dropped their backpacks and began to engage in "the devil's
twitchings." A woman is forbidden to be on the soleas, the candle
seller explained, unless she is being married and is standing next to
her husband. She says she feared the women would enter the altar
or get naked. She continues:*

WITNESS: They had dresses that bared their shoulders and
were very bright in color, and very contrasting! And they
had hats of different colors too. And their tights were different colors! . . . This was blasphemy, sacrilege, and an insult to
my feelings, and my faith, and my ideals, and a defilement
of my personage and my life choice! The pain has not let up.

DEFENSE ATTORNEY: Did you seek psychological or psychiatric help for your suffering?

WITNESS: I am an Orthodox believer. The healing energy
of the Holy Ghost is a million times stronger than any
psychologist.

DEFENSE ATTORNEY: Did the healing energy of the Holy Ghost relieve your moral suffering then?

Judge disallows the question.

. . .

NADYA: Is feminist a swear word?
WITNESS: It is if it's said in church.

. . .

DAY 2

Testimony of witness Vasily Tsyganyuk, altar warden.

WITNESS: Those who are possessed can exhibit different behaviors. They can scream, beat their heads against the floor, jump up and down . . .
DEFENSE ATTORNEY: Do they dance?
WITNESS: Well, no.
JUDGE: Stop questioning him about those who are possessed. Tsyganyuk is not a medical professional and is not qualified to render a diagnosis.

. . .

Testimony of witness, Pavel Zhelezov, altar warden. Witness describes trying to restrain the women. He says one of them broke free and began crossing herself.

JUDGE: Did she cross herself the way all citizens do?

WITNESS: I don't remember exactly. But in essence it was a parody of crossing herself, a satire. People should cross themselves with piety and without rushing. She crossed herself kind of rapidly. This was not the sort of cross with which Orthodox Christians should bless themselves. . . . I did not even watch the clip to the end, because it was filthy. But I noticed something. I used to sing in the choir, and I noticed that their song resembled church music. In other words, this was a parody of a church service, and this is insulting.

. . .

Testimony of witness Sergey Beloglazov, a security guard at the cathedral.

WITNESS: I was traumatized and have been unable to work for two months as a result. Personally, I forgive them. But as far as God and the other faithful are concerned, I cannot make that decision. It is up to God and the court.

NADYA: Do you find the word feminist insulting?

WITNESS: I do. For an Orthodox believer it is an insult, an obscenity.

NADYA: Do you know what the word feminist means?

Judge disallows the question.

. . .

Testimony of Sergey Vinogradov, an electrician at the cathedral.

WITNESS: I arrived at the cathedral at seven in the morning. My office is in one of the pylons. At eleven in the morning I needed to manually throw a switch, so I went downstairs into the upper temple. When I was still in the elevator, I heard women screaming, appealing for help from all believers. Even though I am not a security guard, I was compelled to stand guard for the faith. I saw absolute sacrilege happening on the soleas: They were jumping, flailing their arms, and, finally, dropping to their knees. I was able to join forces with one other man to restrain one of their members who had been on the soleas; I held her down with my left hand. I removed her hat and saw that it was Maria Alyokhina. I escorted her to security and returned to work. I only watched what they were doing for fifteen seconds, but time is relative. Sometimes seconds can seem more than an hour. This was not a performance. It was a witches' ritual. . . . I do not accept their apology. It is insincere and intended for the court. A sincere apology would mean admitting responsibility for the schism, donning fetters, and joining a convent.

. . .

DAY 7

Prosecutor's statement.

PROSECUTOR: The trial has established that Tolokonnikova, Alyokhina, and Samutsevich came to the cathedral on February 21 and inserted themselves into a location reserved for use by Russian Orthodox Church clergy, and stood in a place intended for the reading of scripture. They were dressed in clothing inappropriate for such a place; their arms and shoulders were bare, and they had on face masks in vivid colors with openings for the eyes and mouth. Despite attempts to remove them from the blessed place, they continued to move around in a vulgar, cynical, defiant manner. The accused do not deny having committed these acts. The question is, how should their actions be evaluated?

The prosecution agrees with the preliminary investigation: These actions constituted felony hooliganism. They caused profound insult and humiliation to the faithful. They shouted out curse words that constituted blasphemy. Rules of conduct are determined by the Orthodox tradition and spiritual customs. Bright colors may not be worn, screaming is not allowed, nor is photography or videotaping possible without a special blessing. The reading of prayer and scripture is allowed only as part of a service, or at other times, by special blessing.

As the Russian Orthodox Church has decreed, blasphemy is one of the most severe crimes. The accused acted in such a manner as to maximize pain caused to Orthodox believers. They claim not to have read the cathedral's rules. But those rules should have been obvious to them! They have mocked and challenged Orthodox Christiandom by exerting negative psychoemotional influence on a group of believers. . . . They have violated the rights of the Russian Orthodox Church. . . . They have also attracted the attention of larger society, thereby increasing the impact of their crime. . . . Their guilt is exacerbated by prior planning. Their actions were thought through in advance; each had her own role.

They had rehearsed. . . . A search of Tolokonnikova's residence turned up a brightly colored yellow dress and two face masks, a black one and a blue one, and all of these objects have been admitted as material evidence. . . . We must consider the level of danger they pose to society. We believe that the accused can only be reformed under conditions of incarceration. We ask that they be found guilty and be sentenced to the following. For Tolokonnikova three years of penal colony. For Samutsevich we ask that she be found guilty and sentenced to two years of general-security penal colony. For Alyokhina we ask for three years in a general-security colony.

Closing Statement from
Defense Attorney Violetta Volkova

May it please the court, may it please the participants of the trial: For centuries Russia has preserved its Orthodox traditions. For more than a thousand years it has conserved and proliferated the spiritual heritage of the Orthodox faith, begat to us from the time of Holy Prince Vladimir, Sergius of Radonezh, Patriarch Tikhon. On February 21, 2012, in forty seconds, three girls destroyed the sanctity of everything with a song prayer to the Blessed Virgin. Totally everything. Nothing is hallow!

How shameful, how shameful, how utterly shameful it is for me to listen to the arguments of the public prosecution. There's a sense right now that we're not in twenty-first-century Russia but in some alternate universe in a fairytale like *Alice in Wonderland*, like *Alice Through the Looking-Glass*, and right now this whole ludicrous reality will disappear and crumble like a house of cards. And three imprisoned girls will rise and return home to their families, to their children.

What is the public prosecution's ludicrous stand? How can this circumlocution be publicly and earnestly voiced as the position of the public prosecution? From what law, code of conduct, what instructions (at the very least) did the Ministry of Justice of the Federation draw on for all of these terms: *sacrilege, blasphemy, obscene songs, legs raised in a vulgar way?*

Oh, of course, it's from a letter by the sacristan of the Cathedral of Christ the Savior, Mr. Ryazantsev. It's from a letter by members of the Council of Muftis. It's from the Bishops' Council and two ecumenical councils—Trulsk and Laodicean.

Metropolitan Alexy, the person the prosecution spoke of so devoutly, was not the patriarch, since he never belonged to the Russian Orthodox Church and the Cathedral of Christ the Savior. The upper temple of the Cathedral of Christ the Savior is not a part of the Orthodox Church. I'll repeat myself, it has yet to be handed over to the Russian Orthodox Church. It is used by the Foundation of the Cathedral of Christ the Savior in accordance with its liturgical objectives. But conducting church ceremonies is not a part of the liturgical function of the Foundation of the Cathedral of Christ the Savior.

However, the investigation doesn't want to ascertain these facts. Otherwise, it would seem as though the cultural Orthodox ceremonies held in the upper temple of Christ the Savior are arbitrary. There is no consecrated place in the temple where the prayer—the punk prayer—occurred. There never was.

The upper temple of the Cathedral of Christ the Savior complex is as much an imitation of a house of religious worship as a mannequin is, for instance, an imitation of a person. There are arms, and legs, and there's even a head, but there is no heart or life. Still, neither the investigation nor the public prosecution deemed it necessary to ascertain this; no one raised that question. And no one raised the question: Do the charges fit the crime? No one wants to establish the truth in this case, neither the investigation nor the public prosecution. Otherwise, how else can you explain to Russia and the rest of the world why for five months these women, these innocent women, have been held in custody? They were arrested; they see neither their children nor their families; they do not see the light of day; they are tortured.

What has the public prosecution charged the defendants with? Their clothes were the wrong color. They stood in the wrong place. They didn't pray in the proper manner. They made the sign of the cross in the wrong direction and at the wrong speed. They turned their rears to the Sacred Nail, danced, moving diabolically. They raised their legs in a vulgar way in the sacramental area of the church. I don't misspeak—that's exactly what's written in the state's indictment, read aloud to us by the prosecution. This is how easily they demolished the age-old foundations of the Orthodox faith!

I'll focus briefly only on those procedural violations that we, the defense, have witnessed during the course of this case. While the investigatory process was being conducted, the opinions of the accused, who are now the defendants, and their defense were not once taken into account. Any questions that the defense tried to ask the accused during the investigatory process were struck by this wording: since they won't testify, refused to cooperate with the investigation, refused to plead guilty, then they don't have the right to ask questions.

All of the expert evaluations, conducted by the investigation, were conducted in secret, covertly. There is not one expert evaluation, from the moment the defense decided to conduct it to when a decision was reached, that was agreed upon and accepted by our defendants. It wasn't until later, and in no rush, but after a considerable amount of time had passed after these expert evaluations were conducted that our defendants were informed of the outcomes. Accordingly, they couldn't ask their own questions, or call into question the experts' authority or the experts themselves who conducted the evaluations. Therefore, they could not participate equally in the investigation. This was a violation of equal rights, the adversarial system—fundamental rights according to both the Constitution and international law.

The investigation used persistently a video to build their case, which is, and everyone agrees, a compilation of several different events with a superimposed audio recording. As such, the investigation did not even try to find out who created the video, how it ended up posted on the Internet, and exactly when it happened. Why not? Because the investigation has no use for this information.

Why find answers to these questions? Why do we need expertise to be carried out with authenticity about what really and truly happened in the Cathedral of Christ the Savior? The investigation that took place was a work of fiction. Absolutely everything, including the documents pertaining to the investigation, are part of this work of fiction. Only the victims and witnesses (though not all of the witnesses) spoke of exactly what happened in the Cathedral of Christ the Savior.

We were denied adequate familiarization with the case materials. And it should embarrass anyone in this room that the court subsequently ascertained that there had been enough time. That's not so. The criminal files included seven volumes, thirteen CDs containing video, and five data carriers containing more than one and a half terabytes of data. In order to fully familiarize ourselves with all of the material evidence and the case file at a rate of speed at which electronic information may be reviewed, we estimated that we would need ninety days of nonstop viewing to merely watch all the video files on the those data carriers in our possession, which are attached to the this criminal case.

Our defendants were never allowed to review these materials.

No one made any attempt to show them what they are accused of. What is the reason? Beside the fact that it's impossible to show all of this material evidence in the detention center? Regulations at the detention center forbid bringing in any data carriers or any other kind of technological devices. So, by taking our defendants into custody, the investigation knew in advance that it was violating their right to have access to the case, but they did it anyway. I was not allowed to copy information from the data carriers that are in with the material evidence, data carriers seized from Alekhina, Tolokonnikova, and Pyotr. Verzilov, Tolokonnikova's husband. What's more, the investigation indicates everywhere, for some reason I can't understand, that I'm familiar with all of the material. When signing the protocol on access to the case under Article 217, I stated that I had not been provided with all of the material pertaining to the case, and that I had not been allowed to review all of the material pertaining to the case. But what followed, for some reason, was that the courts and subsequently this present court indicated in relevant motions that had been filed that I had been shown all of the material. I cannot understand why it was necessary to give false information and why, earlier, when we petitioned the court to allow us finally to review the material pertaining to this case and process, the consequence was that the public prosecution paid no attention to the flagrant violation of the law in regard to our defendants.

On the day that the protocols regarding access to material evidence were to be signed, my colleagues Polozov and Feygin were completely shut out of the detention center. When the girls were supposed to sign all of the documents, and I discussed this during the trial, it was in my presence. What's more, it wasn't that they were refusing to sign the corresponding protocols, they just asked, and lawfully so, that their lawyers be present. And they wrote this down on a blank piece of paper, provided to them by the investigation. After that, the corresponding protocols appeared in the case. I witnessed it myself. So don't tell me that all of our defendants' rights have been met. I have witnessed how the investigation forged those corresponding documents.

From the first moments of the trial—from the moment that this case went to trial and from the scheduling of the preliminary hearing in the judicial proceeding—we were not granted even one confidential meeting with our defendants. Not one! Not even an hour to meet confidentially. Saying that we can talk privately with them while in the courtroom is not true. There are always people close by, guards on duty, dogs . . .

Do you think the rights of our defendants have been met?

Is this how the right to privately confer has been met?

Will the public prosecution reproach our defendants that we were not ready to conduct this trial?

We are ready, but our defendants have not had the opportunity to consult with us about the procedure of this process. And the public prosecution did everything to ensure that the rights of our defendants were violated.

Suppressive measures against our defendants are unlawful, without just cause. This is in violation of all the existing rules that relate to the documents and rulings of the Plenum of the Supreme Court of the Russian Federation, which prohibit the selection of this kind of measure of restraint in cases such as these. And the European Court of Human Rights will provide answers and give their own assessment of these illegal activities. Unfortunately, it won't be soon, but I understand with utter clarity and I'm positive of the kind of assessment it will be.

Factually, we as the defense have had no chance of providing normal, adequate, and zealous representation for our defendants. And the opportunity to do so was taken away from us by the court and the public prosecution. For the last two weeks and longer, we have bore witness to the torture and general inhumane and degrading treatment of our defendants. They were not allowed adequate sleep; they were not given enough to eat and were not provided with hot meals. They were humiliated. This, too, will find its assessment in the European Court of Human Rights. The public prosecution crossed the line and made things personal by insulting the defense on a regular basis, from one day in court to the next.

The court prevented due process of the law during the trial by not admitting witnesses and experts who had been invited to the courthouse. It engaged in shutting its doors, and this has been documented for the record by the defense. On August 3, there was an attempt to bar the press and the public from the courtroom while court was in session. This was an attempt to violate the principle of an open trial. And the public prosecution, as the side that is responsible for preserving justice in this case, paid absolutely no attention to it. They closed their eyes.

The principles of the adversarial system, the principle of equality between both parties—these fundamental rules of criminal procedure, were regularly and systematically violated during the proceedings. We perpetually spoke up about these systemic violations of the judicial process in this court every day, literally, nonstop. As a representative of the state, the public prosecution, which is obliged to be a proponent of justice during the process, did not once pay attention to the gross violations of our defendants' rights.

Do you think that a fair trial is being conducted here?

Do you *really* think that this is a court of justice?

Throughout this process it was namely the state, and not the girls, who threw a knockout punch at the Russian Orthodox Church, cynically scoffing at the spiritual traditions of Orthodoxy, the commandments of the Bible. And to my great sorrow, the Russian Orthodox Church will not recover from it soon. Only hourly spiritual ministry to faith, only faith and the Lord will be able to close this gaping, festering wound that exposes a withdrawal of the Russian Orthodox Church, whose face is its primate, its senior clergy, from the spiritual sphere into the sphere of politics, into a close bond between church and state as political institutions, a withdrawal of the church from the sphere of morality, spirituality and faith into politics.

There hasn't been a blasphemy trial in Russia in ninety-five years—not since 1917. In 2012, time turned back to the Middle Ages. Announcing its official position "The Voice of the Church," Archpriest Vsevolod Chaplin, called the patriarch a politician. However, during this entire process we witness the public prosecution's diligent withdrawal from the political sphere to the sphere of the common criminal.

This is not a criminal case.

These women are recognized as political prisoners by international organizations such as Amnesty International, Memorial, and others. These women are not here now because they danced in church in the wrong clothes, in the wrong place, and prayed incorrectly, and made the sign of the cross the wrong way. They are here for their political beliefs. The words of the song, the words of the prayer that they performed—it is a political song, a political prayer addressed to the Blessed Virgin.

From the side I'm on, I've always been surprised by the position of the Russian Orthodox Church. What about the Regulations of the Russian Orthodox Church—Section 9 in particular—which prohibit the church from operating in the political sphere? Why is the patriarch called a politician?

There is no answer to this question. We see a growing union, a tandem between the state and the Russian Orthodox Church, the government's withdrawal from the secular into clericalism. That nail, which it is sinful to turn your back on, it's now the nail hammered into the Constitution and the law, and they are bleeding, here, in this court of justice.

The church is becoming a state institution, while the Constitution which is basic law, is increasingly being transformed into a monument. A monument that stands on the graves of law, justice, and human rights, all of which were made a mockery of in the most egregious manner, violated through the process of this trial and throughout this case.

Closing Statement by
Defense Attorney Mark Feygin

How did this case begin? On February 21, 2012, during the political elections, our defendants went to the Cathedral of Christ the Savior as if they were going to a political direct action, and they took part in a political direct action. It was definitely outrageous and hugely nonconformist. Certainly not everyone shares their point of view about the choice of time and place.

Nevertheless, I, as a lawyer for Nadezhda Tolokonnikova, representing the interests in this case as they pertain to the incriminating Article 213, Part 2, along with the other representatives of the defense, thought from the very beginning that the act committed was not a criminal offense. Of course, it wasn't. Because from the very beginning the lawyers, and even just informed people, could easily perceive that it was an administrative offense. This has been discussed many, many, many times. The main indicator that separates our defendants from the incriminating Article 213, Part 2, "hooliganism committed by a group of persons, premeditated and motivated by religious hatred and enmity" is the bias of the act committed.

The bias of this so-called criminal act was never against the public. Never. This is an imperative qualifying attribute of the corpus delicti of Article 213, Part 2. We, the defense team, said from the very beginning that it should be categorized as an administrative offense per Article 5.26 of the Administrative Offense Code. This is a violation of the law pertaining to freedom of conscience, religion, and religious association. Part 2 absolutely fits with the characteristics of the act committed according to these main points: it is an insult to the religious sensitivities of the citizen, or the desecration of revered items, signs, and emblems, which are ideologically symbolic. In this case, the action without a doubt leaned toward an administrative offense and it was far from being a public matter; instead it was an encroachment on the citizen's individual constitutional right to freedom of conscience.

And really, if you look at it objectively, would these acts committed by our defendants be qualified the same way if they had occurred in, let's just say, the Arbat? A place where people dance, jump around, make faces, perform wearing strange clothes, throw their legs in the air the very same way that has been described here many times. With their choreography they probably would not have collected much money. . . . At the same time, you see, the definition of an act pertaining to the public presupposes, first of all, that it is public regardless of time and place. What this means is, the act committed must be dangerous to the public, not just in a church but anywhere—in the street, in a theater, in the Arbat, which I just mentioned. Why? Because the element that qualifies something as hooliganism is its violent nature. The violent nature of the acts committed. Everything that happened at the pretrial investigation and at the trial itself proves that those acts did not have a violent nature.

I will talk about defendants Tolokonnikova, Alyokhina, and Samutsevich together, as this pertains to Article 213, Part 2. Not only did they show absolutely no aggression, but they also showed absolutely no resistance in spite of what's been said here, and the video testifies to this fact without prejudice. There was never any use of force, never any show of resistance in the defendants' actions. None. They parted easily with the items the guards took from them on the spot. They parted with them voluntarily, in spite of their yelling, which was simply recitative speech acts. They voluntarily left the *bemata*, which is comprised of the solea and *ambo*.

What more can be said about how it's possible to stretch the restrictions of public life and question what is criminal in this case? They voluntarily proceeded to the exit without any resistance. Not to mention that the private security company Kolokol has instructions to take definitive action, to not allow any activities dangerous to the public in the church. The guards of that private security company Kolokol did nothing to detain them, as they've said here in the court; they did not give the order to close the gates of the cathedral and hand over to law enforcement those persons who committed publically dangerous acts. And why? Because there was no crime committed. There was an administrative offense, which in essence can be easily identified on the basis of its own parts.

Please, let's look at this incident impartially. There was an incident, but again, there was no violent nature to it. Throughout the whole pretrial investigation, we argued that it's impossible to drag a video clip proving motive of religious hatred and malice over to the prosecutorial side. The investigation rigidly insisted that this performance art can be taken as a foundation on which it's possible to build proof of Item B of Article 213, Part 2, "the motive is religious hatred and enmity toward a religious group of Orthodox believers."

Indeed, it's already been discussed that the clip was not investigated. Neither those who made it nor those who released it are mentioned in the case materials. What's more, our defendants said at their interrogation that they are neither the authors, nor its creators, nor the initiators of it being published on the Internet. This matter has not been proven in the criminal case. It wasn't investigated at all. It was also not investigated during the trial because of various excuses. First they said that it's not the subject of the criminal investigation in this criminal case. Then they said that in and of itself it proves that these actions were of a reoccurring nature—that they could be amassed, collected into something circumstantial which qualifies as the corpus delicti of the crime, Part 2 of Article 213. But we still haven't heard a clear and accurate position regarding what the requirements are for it being used by the prosecution.

It turns out that the motive can be easily established by the attitudes of several victims, who testified here about this action. It's necessary to say that they differ notwithstanding the general unity of their position. At some point, Potankin, while giving a primary explanation of the events at the cathedral, announced that the incident didn't affect him at all; later he changed his testimony. Of course many of those people are Orthodox believers. I feel much sympathy for Beloglazov. Certainly, people who wanted a chance to also show their humanitarian regard for our defendants did so by speaking about it with complete openness. However, the degree of the victims' suffering was not proven by the evidence. Not one had to go see a doctor. We still have not determined what the moral damage was, although the court was obliged to do so. In no uncertain terms is there enough to prove the prosecutory side of this case per Article 213, Part 2, according to the attitudes of that group.

All right, there were experts in the case. This is crucial. There are three expert evaluations in the sixth volume of the case. The first expert evaluation was conducted almost immediately, at the end of February. The examination was conducted by the State Unitary Enterprise Center for Information and Analytical Technologies. Everything's legal. The materials available for the case at that time are also presented. They have to present their case, so, they present their case. Those people who are specialists at the State Unitary Enterprise Center for Information and Analytical Technologies—psychologists and linguists—conducted an expert evaluation and determined that there was practically no claim to this expert evaluation. They only answered yes to the fourth question, that there had indeed been an insult, but that it was of an administrative nature. This was conducted by former legal investigator Tsedov of the Khamovnichesky Department of Internal Affairs.

The case, from what we know, is presented again, at the very beginning of March, to the Internal Affairs Department of the Central District. The case is taken up by legal investigator Ranchenkov. He has a feeling that something's not adding up. So something has to be done. The components of Article 213, Part 2 can't be teased out. So let's create a supplemental expert evaluation. Let's make the questions more direct. That way there will be enough to meet the requirements of Article 213, Part 2. He sends the new questions to the State Unitary Enterprise Center for Information and Analytical Technologies. Legal investigator Ranchenkov, who investigates this case in the context of Article 213, Part 2, raised no questions pertaining to Article 282, absolutely not one about how the spiritual elements of this article cannot be put to a psychological and linguistic expert evaluation. Psychological and linguistic expert evaluations answer concrete questions, but not about what qualifies as a crime. It must be assessed in and of itself. And he cannot, as a matter of fact, regardless of what questions are asked, give a straight answer about qualification, or which article of the criminal code can serve as the basis for the answers to those incriminating questions. The expert evaluations don't fit either.

The answer comes on May 16. Even before the results were in, the legal investigator understood that Article 213 didn't apply; it just didn't fit. So they get their own people. They gather their own experts, who will write whatever's required of them. They reach an agreement with anyone they possibly can: the victims' lawyers pull in people who are seemingly close to the foundation of the Cathedral of Christ the Savior. They chose the necessary people—three experts, who'll write what's needed, but since they're in a hurry, since time is short, they phrase the questions pertaining to motive directly, which, according to the law pertaining to state judicial evaluation activity, is not allowed.

The questions must be phrased solely within the scope of the psychological and linguistic, and cannot be based on judicial requirements. They cannot be directly about motive, because that question is to be determined judicially in court. They phrased the questions directly. There was no time. They had to close the case. They were in a hurry.

So the experts yield, sign the documents, answer, "Yes, there was motive present" to everything. Forget about this being a gross violation—one lawyer who took part in the expert evaluation had no right to do so, seeing as he's connected with one of the victims' attorneys. It's clear that this group of people fabricated expert evaluations. Why are they doing this? So that the case will hold up; they have to make it hold up. This doesn't add up, that doesn't add up, but they must incarcerate, understand? Since the order to incarcerate came down from high above, they must send them away.

The story continues. So, they've done their expert evaluations. The defense makes every attempt to have this evidence ruled inadmissible. Our remarks and motions pertaining to the improper nature of these evaluations, which have been conducted with prejudice, are in Volume 6 of the trial transcripts.

On May 23, a nondisclosure agreement is signed, although it should have been done on the fourteenth, when the expert evaluations started. This is a gross procedural violation. It means that outside material was used. It means that it's unclear who participated in the preparation of this expert evaluation. It could have been conducted anywhere, by any organization. But there's an order, a political order, to incarcerate. Do you understand? So they proceed. Everything works out, everything holds up.

You may ask yourself, why such prejudice? Where is this conclusion coming from? Let's take eyewitness Ugrik, who takes the stand here while court is in session and recounts that legal investigator Ranchenkov doesn't only work at his legal responsibilities investigating this case, but as you know, he also works in television. You know that he refers select victims and witnesses to appear on channel RTR, on Mamontov's show *Provocateurs*. How, after all, can the interests of the investigation of the case be upheld if the investigator works in television? What's next? Are they going to build a show around the materials of this criminal case? Is someone with his legal status even allowed to do this? What does this testify to? That it's a closed circle of people, a closed circle that's busying itself with the incarceration of three young women.

It's all because of this order, which is political. This entire case from beginning to end is political. The accused in this case, our clients, now the defendants who are facing real time, they are the political opposition, who decided to use nonconformist tactics to express their attitude regarding the concordance between the church and the state, which is an authoritarian state. Much of what they did looked clumsy and excessively shocking. Many found it unacceptable. However, the criminal code has no place here; the criminal code has no jurisdiction here.

Throughout the course of the entire investigation and the indictment that followed here in this court, there was a constant usage of terminology by the participants of the trial that conveyed a purely theological disposition. Occasionally, the criminal law was tainted by it, but what's most amazing is that no one understands why the Constitution is secular in nature. Why is the state secular in nature? Why doesn't it occur to anyone to ask the question: Why isn't Russia a theocratic state? This isn't just a historical question, nor is it a question of civilization in general. The standard functions of the Constitution are labeled as secular and allow for the "nonexistence" of God, to phrase it delicately, because it operates in the world of physical phenomena, you see? If we allow for the existence of God in the Constitution then standards and structures that are canonical in nature may be extrapolated to the criminal code, but civilization and the world have already lived through that kind of state and have handed over the sphere of a relationship with God exclusively to the person, the individual, who accordingly allows him or herself the belief in God.

Among those here, there are many believers, but that does not mean that canonical standards may be inextricably linked with the criminal code. There is no such construct as blasphemy; there is no such construct as sacrilege. These are not the standards of the criminal code. To apply them to the actions of the defendants is virtually impossible.

Following this argument, in a strictly legal sense, it's not just about the decision to indict, but I fear that this may migrate over to the verdict, which in principle is unlawful. We cannot prove anything in this world on the basis of abstract theories, ephemeral conclusions of the mind, on the assumption of the existence of God. God is a separate, completely personal category, which as an absolute is connected exclusively with a person's inner world. [S]He cannot be branded according to the sum of all people's inner lives and then be hatched into existence. We don't have the ability to do this because of the limitations of our conscience. We are incapable of applying our conscience to the task of creating a physical body for that being, that higher being.

That's why, for instance, my belief in God, Violetta or Kolya's, or that of any other random person, cannot be imperative. This must be understood. And it's namely the strength of these reasons that the law, the legal system, which is founded on secular standards, cannot allow for religious interpretation. Humankind has been down that road. And it seems there's no going back. It's impossible, operating only under the belief in God, to explain the travels of the Mars Rover, as it takes photographs and does so much more. Just the same, the rules of humankind cannot explain the infinity of the universe. That's why people who try to explain everything according to canonical standards, no matter what, are either lying or completely obtuse.

This is why, I'd like to say, that we cannot try our defendants in this criminal case; the trial cannot judge while operating exclusively—here I emphasize, exclusively—on the basis of this theocratic understanding of the law. The secular nature of the government presupposes that even in church there can be no blasphemous deeds committed, but administrative and criminal acts. This is precisely spelled out in the law. It's there in the administrative law and the criminal law.

When the Constitution is rewritten so that it speaks to the theocratic nature of the government, at that point we can hold a trial based on theocratic law, but that is not what we have now. So we are obliged to hold a trial according to the standards that maximally apply to the assessment of our defendants' actions. With the exception of Article 5.26 of the Administrative Code, the corresponding text of which I've already indicated, there's no other component that plugs into the aspects of this act.

I would also like to point out that Russia has already passed that period, that Synodal period in Russia's history, starting from Peter the Great and ending in a return to patriarchy, and that period was pernicious. By the way, in this period, more so than at any other time, there was a shortage of saints in the church. It's a well-known fact. The church had merged with the government so tightly that, in part or in whole, it brought on the catastrophe of 1917. And if both the church and the government should return today to that which they have already left behind, then we are in danger of reverting and plunging Russia right back into that very same situation.

Why did this trial take on such a sweeping scope? After all, they're three random women, who the prosecution has presented as hooligans, governed by hooliganistic motives, who, come what may, wished to proclaim their feminist position, or whatever else it may have been. So why did this trial attract such attention? There is one more explanation, one that's very important. It's because so many people saw the lawlessness. It's because lawlessness reigns in Russia. There is no justice in Russia. In Russia, if you're the accused, never mind if you're under investigation, it's considered appropriate to lick the judge's boots. Not only are you supposed to apologize, as was expected of our defendants, and not only are you supposed to repent. You're supposed to confess to absolutely everything. You're supposed to cry, grovel. You're supposed to completely crush your own personality. You're supposed to give the government the opportunity to tear you to pieces. You're supposed to turn into a complete nothing, and only at that point is it possible for you to earn something close to leniency.

Nothing has changed since the Soviet years. People can expect humane treatment only by completely annihilating their own identities. When the government bumped up against these personalities—and I can personally attest that at the preliminary hearing, my defendants were not only expected to be repentant, not only to be apologetic to the Orthodox, which they could have done easily and in fact have done, they apologized in no uncertain terms and immediately to all those who they believe they have insulted—the defendants had no desire to offend the faithful. The entire time, the legal investigator kept saying, they must repent. They must turn to nothing. They must make it so that everyone will see that in the face of the government they are nothing, that they're not capable of withstanding having their freedom taken from them. Only then do they have some specter of a chance: a special deal, a suspended sentence.

But suddenly, the defendants said, no, that's not how it's going to be. A human being has enough worth that she should be shown respect by the inquest, the court, and the government. We are representatives of a free society.

That's what they said. And that's exactly how we defended them, as free citizens.

I conclude by saying that the government turned up nothing. They turned up nothing. They did not manage to crush the identities of our defendants, who made not one compromise that would go against their consciences. I sincerely believe that at the moment in history when on Via Dolorosa He had to carry the cross, these three would have helped him without hesitation, just as those who have sought revenge and the cruelest of punishments against them would have not. For there is more Christianity in them than in many of those who seek to condemn them. And that is why I know that they have committed no crime and should be acquitted. What's more, if the government, using this trial as its public face, should move to send them away for a specified period of time, it will signify that a return to this present way of life will never again be possible. It will cause a rift between the people and the government once and for all. When all is said and done, the people will never forgive the government for committing such a crime against the innocent.

Closing Statement by
Defense Attorney Nikolay Polozov

May it please the court, may it please the participants of the trial: My colleagues have probably said it all. Let me add a few things. First of all, our defendants stand accused—I'm not talking about the formal charges, but speaking in general—of disorderly conduct and violating the rules observed in church. They are accused of perpetrating blasphemy and sacrilege, and although these words only partly come across in the indictment, everyone understands that the accusation pertains exclusively to them.

I would like to mention the so-called butterfly effect. Unfortunately, there are moments, when a point of no return is reached. Once the prosecution pursued a criminal procedure for an offense the defendants did not commit, we reached a point of no return, a butterfly effect.

Let's go back a little. As our defendants have said, literally less than a year ago the group Pussy Riot was formed. The goal of this group was to bring across artistic forms of political protest to the broadest stratum of the public. They did this successfully. At first their fame was—let's be honest—insignificant, with the exception of a narrow circle of sympathizers and followers of actionism in contemporary art who admired their creative work. But, thanks to television, thanks to the aid of mass media, thanks to the efforts of the government above all else, their activities became known to the entire world. There's probably not a corner of the world that doesn't know what the group Pussy Riot is.

The point of no return occurred at the moment when the decision was made to prosecute our defendants for the act, which, as my colleagues have rightfully discussed, was just a minor administrative offense. It's true, the devout have been insulted. I, as a religious person, am insulted, although my opinion at this trial is not decisive. The performance at the Cathedral of Christ the Savior was probably a bit too much, even from an artistic point of view. But it is not a criminal offense and it cannot be considered one in principle, because we have a constitution. And here I would like to turn to the Constitution.

My colleagues, the opposing side, have already brought this up. Unfortunately, for some, the Constitution has become nothing more than letters written in a book. Unfortunately, our government, which is obliged to uphold the Constitution and to monitor that it is upheld by all of the citizens and people who reside in the territories of the Russian Federation, does not always observe it. There's a growing sense that the Constitution has been forgotten. But this Constitution was adopted by our nation, which withstood tremendous suffering. It was adopted after more than seventy years of the Soviet system, the camps of the Gulag, the Patriotic War, the Great Patriotic War, and at the cost of the lives of millions of people, people who endeavored so that we, and our descendents, would live justly and with dignity.

The second half of Article 4 of the Constitution says that

the Constitution of the Russian Federation and federal law is supreme throughout the entire territory of the Russian Federation. The Constitution makes no exception. Its jurisdiction is absolutely the same in the home as it is in the street, the railway station, the mosque, and the cathedral. There are no exceptions. This means that even in the Cathedral of Christ the Savior, the Constitution of the Russian Federation holds the same jurisdiction that it does in any other place, in the entire territory of the Russian Federation, from Kaliningrad to Vladivostok.

In addition, there is Article 13. What does it address? It says that the Russian Federation recognizes ideological diversity, and that means that a person may profess any ideological views as long as they do not contradict the Constitution. Even if it's feminism, which is what our defendants spoke of. Feminism is not a blasphemous curse, as some people seem to think. Feminism is an ideology, and its believers have absolutely the same rights as believers of Russian Orthodoxy or Judaism or Communism. Absolutely the same rights, as long as they do not violate the Constitution. In this case, as we can see, the ideology of our defendants does not violate the Constitution.

Let's continue. Article 14 of the Constitution says that the Russian Federation is a secular government and that no religion may be established as federal or compulsory. I fully support the outlook of those people who wrote this Constitution—our people. We live in a multinational, interfaith country. A very big country—the biggest country in this entire world. We know that in order for us to all get along, people must be able to have their own beliefs. People try to defend their beliefs. But in order for us to all to live together, we must have some core common value. And this core is precisely the principle of the secular, the principle that government remains equidistant from any and every religion and ideology.

Unfortunately, in recent times, the government has moved toward violating the Constitution. Preference is granted to certain religious figures. What might this lead to? It can have very bad consequences. It can lead to civil war. It can lead to the destruction of our government. I'm certain that not one reasonable person who lives in the Russian Federation wants this scenario.

Part 2 of Article 14 talks about how religious organizations are separate from the government and equal under the law. Not one religious organization can hold itself above the law or above any other religious organizations. But here too, unfortunately, very unpleasant exceptions do occur. I will once again return to the Constitution. We have repeatedly heard references made to various regulations—religious and church regulations. The Council of Trullo, the Council of Laodicea, and other decrees have been accepted as public organizations from a judicial point of view.

Part 3 of Article 15 says that laws are subject to official publication, that unpublished laws do not apply. Regulatory acts that affect the rights and freedoms of a citizen cannot be applied if the laws are not published officially for public knowledge.

Where can we see the published laws of the Council of Trullo? Why is it being referenced? Why isn't the Constitution being referred to, while totally ancient regulations are? No doubt, these councils—these judicial, religious monuments—have a right to exist, and they belong with the research of specialists. The Code of Hammurabi, for example, in no way indicates how we should live now. According to this code, your hands should be cut off for theft. This does not correspond to our contemporary understanding of humanism, to our values.

We are on a serious course leading to the Code of Hammurabi. Why do we need the Constitution? In Article 19, the government guarantees equal rights and freedom to a person regardless of gender, race, nationality, language, origin, ownership of property and vocation, place of residence, religious orientation, or beliefs. Any form of restriction to the rights of the citizen on the basis of social, race, national, language, and religious association are forbidden.

We were told that every monastery has its own charter here. But we know that the Constitution should be applied to every territory in all of Russia. Undoubtedly, it's necessary to respect those ceremonies, those traditions that exist in any religion. But, if you'll allow me, why is there such a drastic differentiation between men and women, who are kept separate? Why are some allowed to walk in and practice certain observances in a specified place, but others are not? Yes, I understand, this matter touches on the inner workings of a religion. An agreement is reached within that society, which makes such customs possible. They agree, for example, that women don't belong in certain places and men do. But what we have here isn't a church trial; what we have here is secular. Our trial is being conducted according to secular laws . . .

Judge Syrova interrupts

. . . our trial is being conducted according to the Criminal Procedure Code, according to the Criminal Code. Let's continue. We don't have to go far. Everything's written in the Constitution.

An individual's human dignity is protected by the government. No one should be exposed to torture. We have already discussed torture. Torture is covered in the [Geneva] Convention under the protection of human rights but, unfortunately, torture was used here. Our defendants did not eat or drink; they were not allowed to sleep. What else can we call this but torture? Yes, it's true that they weren't strung up on a rack. Those days are over. But something tells me that it's fully possible for time to turn back and soon racks will appear in the courtyards of quiet police detention centers. Why not?

Let's talk about Article 28. Everyone is guaranteed the freedom of conscience, freedom of religious affiliation including the right to worship, either individually or together with other people, any religion, or to worship none, to choose freely, to possess and disseminate different religious beliefs and to act in accordance with them.

But what do we see here? A process is occurring whereby religious views are being imposed on a broad strata of society. Why is this being done? People should go to church only of their own volition. They shouldn't be dragged there. Look at the circumstances in this case—not everyone wants to go there. People are starting to think: Why are we told one thing, but in reality something quite different is happening? People are told to forgive, to love, but in reality a prison sentence is demanded of those who have their own convictions. Why is this happening?

Article 44 is a good part of the Constitution. Everyone is guaranteed the freedom of literary, artistic, scientific, technical, and other forms of creative pursuits and their teachings. But what do we see? We have a punk band. Yes, these young ladies make music, they make art, they make action art. But at some point the government decided that they make it badly, and that it's not permitted. That people like them should not be allowed out on the street. After all, we understand that the controversy does not pertain only to the situation in which the public order was violated in the Cathedral of Christ the Savior. It's very important to understand a principle of proportion here. Unfortunately, this principle of proportion in terms of crime and punishment is totally lacking. We see that for a minor offense, for violating the public order, the prosecution is demanding years, *years* of prison time. How is this possible? All of the victims, in one way or another, as they've said in their testimonies, were fulfilling what can be considered their duties or utilitarian responsibilities. No one was praying; there was no religious service at that moment. No one violated the order of prayer. Who are our victims? The candle seller, the alter boys, the guards. Well, there's one citizen who came to buy icons, as he's testified. But at that moment no one was praying. There is not one citizen among the witnesses who testified saying, I was praying, and Pussy Riot came along and disturbed my prayer. No, everyone was at work. Everyone was fulfilling their vocational obligations. Citizen Istomin came in to buy some icons, but he wasn't praying either. He didn't mention that fact. For this reason, how can it be said that their order was violated? Everyone was busy doing their jobs. Yes, someone couldn't count money after it all happened. Yes, someone had intimations of difficulty with their moral compass, but no one testified to that. Everyone said, yes, there we were . . . No one even said that they felt sick afterward. They said, we're morally insulted. Please forgive me, but an insult to the feelings of believers? That's part of the administrative articles. It's not a criminal offense. It's not punishable by three years, which the prosecution is asking for. That's impossible!

Let's continue. The Constitution's not finished yet.

Consider Article 48 of the Constitution. Everyone is guaranteed the right to receive qualified legal assistance. Our defendants and my colleagues have spoken of the fact that during this trial they were not permitted to confer in private. How can attorneys talk with their clients in the presence of guards, bailiffs, and that dog? How is it possible? We were told, please, come on Friday during the second half of the day, when the police detention center is closed. Yes, one our colleagues, Mark Zakharovich, managed to get in there, but that does not mean that our clients' rights, as stipulated in the Constitution, were observed. It means that they threw us a bone: Well, go on, confer. So to say that the defense and our clients prepared for this trial is false. We neither slept nor ate. We prepared for this trial exceeding our resources because the government, the state, did everything to make sure that we were not prepared; they did everything to keep us from presenting our point of view. They did everything so that we could not present decisive arguments, ones that are admissible and accurate. But we're here, and we are arguing.

Take Article 49 of the Constitution: irremediable uncertainty about the guilt of a person is determined in favor of the accused. In this case, the defendants.

This case is one big irremediable uncertainty. Nothing's been proven. Nothing more than something theological. Nothing in actuality; no regulations have been cited. What did they violate? The rules of the Council of Trullo? But we've already determined that in the Cathedral of Christ the Savior just as in every territory of the Russian Federation, the rules of Council of Trullo do not apply. The Constitution of the Russian Federation holds jurisdiction, and these rules of the Council Trullo are a monument to jurisprudence and religion.

Article 55: the main rights and freedoms listed in the Constitution of the Russian Federation shall not be interpreted as the negation or detract from other generally recognized rights and freedoms of the person and the citizen. But this criminal case shows that there is a total negation of any and all human and civil rights when it comes to upholding the rights of our defendants. No rights are being observed. The fact that they are in the police detention center should in no way permit the state the right to mistreat, torture, demand a confession or repentance. They've apologized, and many of the victims have forgiven them. The majority of the victims, I would say, have forgiven them. Unfortunately, no one has asked my opinion, but as a religious person, I also forgive them, because our Lord Jesus Christ commanded precisely that we forgive and love, not pursue and prosecute.

The first Cathedral of Christ the Savior, the one that was demolished, existed as a monument to the Russian people who were victims of the Patriotic War of 1812. On the walls of that cathedral were the names of those who laid down their lives for our Motherland on the battlefield—at the Battle of Borodino, at Smolensk, and so on. The name of my own forefather was there—Prince Mikhail Vasilyevich Trutsky, General of the Russian Army. In contrast, the things that go on in this building now insult my feelings as a believer. Why are banquets and corporate parties held at the Cathedral of Christ the Savior? And how does that relate to the case of three women who stepped onto the *ambo*, who did not set foot in the altar because it would be a violation of church statute, punishable by three years? Why hasn't the group Boney M., who wiggled around diabolically and sang obscene songs ten meters from the altar, been punished with three years? Why isn't that happening? Why such discrimination? Because the former are foreigners, they can't be prosecuted. They don't speak out against Putin.

Our defendants have said that all their performances were developed within the framework of political protest. Those actions on trolleys, in the metro, at Lobnoye Mesto—all of that was within the framework of political protest. Yes, it goes without saying that the prosecution, that the court, don't want to see the underlying political causes. This trial of ours has veered to the side of clerical interests, but why didn't the investigation examine the history of the band? Why is the whole of its oeuvre being judged according to just one episode? Why did the investigation not study their performance at Lobnoye Mesto, or other places, their writings, what they sing about? They consistently bring across their position that no politics and no bureaucratic functionary may refute the interests of government. That they act in their own interests and that many people in this country do not like these turn of events. But denying the general, the investigation chooses the most particular, only that which fits in with the prosecution's storyline. This selective argument cannot prevail. There must be objectivity in any case, but the investigation has no use for that. It is better to get on every television channel and talk about what blasphemers the defendants are than to realistically address the problems that our nation has amassed.

Well, what else can I say about the Constitution? Two

more Articles—I won't take much more of your time, respected court.

In Article 120 of the Constitution, judges shall be independent and are subordinated only to the Constitution of the Russian Federation and federal law. And in Article 123, the trial shall be conducted on an adversarial and impartial basis. Unfortunately, the way that our trial has been conducted has made me question whether that conduct was properly exercised. Blatant violations were allowed. My colleague Violetta Volkova already spoke in detail about the violations of the court in reviewing this case. A judge must remain objective, impartial, and independent. Every decision delivered by the judge is either a bargain made with conscience or the observance of the law. That's why I ask the respected court to render a verdict governed exclusively by the Constitution of the Russian Federation and federal law.

I ask for full acquittal.

Closing Courtroom Statement by Katya

In the closing statement, the defendant is expected to repent, express regret for her deeds, or enumerate attenuating circumstances. In my case, as in the case of my colleagues in this group, this is completely unnecessary. Instead, I want to voice some thoughts about what has happened to us.

That the Cathedral of Christ the Savior has become a significant symbol in the political strategy of authorities was clear to many thinking people when Vladimir Putin's former [KGB] colleague Kirill Gundyaev took over as leader of the Russian Orthodox Church. After this happened, the Cathedral of Christ the Savior began to be used openly as a flashy backdrop for the politics of the security forces, which are the main source of political power in Russia.

Why did Putin feel the need to exploit the Orthodox religion and its aesthetic? After all, he could have employed his own, far more secular tools of power—for example, the state-controlled corporations, or his menacing police system, or his obedient judicial system. It may be that the harsh, failed policies of Putin's government, the incident with the submarine Kursk, the bombings of civilians in broad daylight, and other unpleasant moments in his political career forced him to ponder whether it was high time to resign; that otherwise, the citizens of Russia would help him do this. Apparently, it was then that he felt the need for more persuasive, transcendent guarantees of his long tenure at the pinnacle of power. It was then that it became necessary to make use of the aesthetic of the Orthodox religion, which is historically associated with the heyday of Imperial Russia, where power came not from earthly manifestations such as democratic elections and civil society, but from God Himself.

How did Putin succeed in this? After all, we still have a secular state, and any intersection of the religious and political spheres should be dealt with severely by our vigilant and critically minded society. Right? Here apparently, the authorities took advantage of a certain absence of the Orthodox aesthetic in Soviet times, an era when the Orthodox religion had an aura of lost history, of something that had been crushed and damaged by the Soviet totalitarian regime, and was thus representative of an opposition culture. The current authorities decided to appropriate this historical effect of loss, and present a new political project to restore Russia's lost spiritual values, a project that has little to do with a genuine concern for the preservation of Russian Orthodoxy's history and culture.

It was also fairly logical that the Russian Orthodox Church, given its long mystical ties to power, emerged as the project's principal proponent in the media. It was decided that, unlike in the Soviet era when the church opposed, above all, the brutality of the authorities toward history itself, the Russian Orthodox Church should now confront all pernicious manifestations of contemporary mass culture and its concepts of diversity and tolerance.

Implementing this thoroughly interesting political project has required considerable quantities of professional lighting and video equipment, airtime on national television for hours-long live broadcasts, and numerous background shoots for morally and ethically edifying news stories, during which the patriarch's well-constructed speeches would in fact, be presented, thus helping the faithful to make the correct political choice during a difficult time for Putin preceding the election. Moreover, the filming must be continuous. The necessary images must be burned into popular memory and constantly updated; they must create the impression of something natural, constant, and compulsory.

Our sudden musical appearance in the Cathedral of Christ the Savior with the song "Virgin Mary, Put Putin Away" violated the integrity of the media image that the authorities had spent such a long time generating and maintaining, and revealed its falsity. In our performance we dared, without seeking the patriarch's blessing, to unite the visual imagery of Orthodox culture with that of protest culture, thus suggesting that Orthodox culture belongs not only to the Russian Orthodox Church, the patriarch, and Putin, but that it could also ally itself with civic rebellion and the spirit of protest in Russia.

Perhaps the unpleasant, far-reaching effect of our media intrusion into the cathedral was even a surprise to the authorities themselves. At first, they tried to present our performance as a prank pulled by heartless, militant atheists. This was a serious blunder on their part, because by then we were already known as an anti-Putin feminist punk band that carried out its media assaults on the country's major political symbols.

In the end, considering all the irreversible political and symbolic losses caused by our innocent creativity, the authorities decided to protect the public from us and our nonconformist thinking. Thus ended our complicated punk adventure in the Cathedral of Christ the Savior.

I now have mixed feelings about this trial. On the one hand, we expect a guilty verdict. Compared to the judicial machine, we are nobodies, and we have lost.

On the other hand, we have won. The whole world now sees that the criminal case against us has been fabricated. The system cannot conceal the repressive nature of this trial. Once again, the world sees Russia differently than the way Putin tries to present it at his daily international meetings. Clearly, none of the steps Putin promised to take toward instituting the rule of law have been taken. And his statement that this court will be objective and hand down a fair verdict is yet another deception presented to the entire country and the international community.

Closing Courtroom Statement by Nadya

By and large, the three members of Pussy Riot are not the ones on trial here. If we were, this event would hardly be so significant. This is a trial of the entire political system of the Russian Federation, which, to its great misfortune, enjoys showing the state's cruelty toward the individual, and its indifference toward human honor and dignity, repeating all of the worst moments of Russian history. To my deep regret, this poor excuse for a judicial process approaches Stalin's troikas. We too have only an interrogator, a judge, and a prosecutor. Furthermore, this repressive act is based on political orders from above that completely dictate the words, deeds, and decisions of these three judicial figures.

What was behind our performance at the Cathedral of Christ the Savior and the subsequent trial? Nothing other than the autocratic political system. Pussy Riot's performances can either be called dissident art, or political action that engages art forms. Either way, our performances are a kind of civic activity amidst the repressions of a corporate political system that directs its power against basic human rights, and civil and political liberties. The young people who have been flayed by the systematic eradication of freedoms perpetrated during the aughts have now risen against the state. We were searching for real sincerity and simplicity, and we found these qualities in the *yurodstvo* [the holy foolishness] of punk.

Passion, total honesty, and naïveté are superior to the hypocrisy, mendacity, and false modesty that are used to disguise crime. The so-called leading figures of our state stand in the cathedral with righteous faces on, but, through their cunning, their sin is greater than our own. We put on political punk performances in response to a government that is rife with rigidity, reticence, and caste-like hierarchical structures. It is so clearly invested in serving only narrow corporate interests, it makes us sick just to breathe Russian air. We categorically oppose the following, and this forces us to act and live politically: The use of coercive and forceful methods for regulating social processes, a situation in which the most important political institutions are the disciplinary structures of the state; the security agencies (the army, police, and secret services) and their corresponding means of ensuring political "stability" (prisons, pre-emptive detention, all the mechanisms of strict control over the citizenry); forcibly imposed civic passivity among the majority of the population; the complete dominance of the executive branch over the legislative and judicial branches.

Moreover, we are deeply frustrated by the scandalous dearth of political culture, which comes as the result of fear and is kept down through the conscious efforts of the government and its servants (Patriarch Kirill: "Orthodox Christians do not attend rallies"), and by the scandalous weakness of horizontal ties within our society. We do not like that the state so easily manipulates public opinion by means of its strict control over the majority of media outlets (a particularly vivid example of this manipulation is the unprecedentedly insolent and distorted campaign against Pussy Riot appearing in practically every Russian media outlet).

Despite the fact that we find ourselves in an essentially authoritarian situation, living under authoritarian rule, I see this system crumbling in the face of three members of Pussy Riot. What the system anticipated did not occur. Russia does not condemn us, and with each passing day, more and more people believe in us and believe that we should be free, and not behind bars. I see this in the people I meet. I meet people who work for the system, who work in its institutions; I see people who are incarcerated. Every day I meet our supporters who wish us luck and, above all, freedom. They say what we did was justified. More and more people tell us that although they earlier had doubts about whether we had the right to do what we did, with each passing day, more and more people tell us that time has shown that our political gesture was correct—that we opened the wounds of this political system, and struck directly at the hornet's nest, so they came after us, but we . . .

These people try to relieve our suffering as much they can, and we are very grateful to them. We are also grateful to everyone who speaks out in support of us on the outside. There are many supporters, and I know it. I know that a great number of Orthodox Christians speak out on our behalf, the ones who gather near the court in particular. They pray for us; they pray for the imprisoned members of Pussy Riot. We've seen the little booklets the Orthodox hand out that contain prayers for the imprisoned. This fact alone demonstrates that there is no single, unified group of Orthodox believers, as the prosecutor would like to insist. Such a unified group does not exist. Today, more and more believers have come to the defense of Pussy Riot. They don't think that what we did warrants a five-month term in a pretrial detention center, let alone the three years in prison the prosecutor has called for.

Every day, more people come to understand that if the system is attacking with such vehemence the three young women who performed in the Cathedral of Christ the Savior for forty seconds, it only means that this system fears the truth, sincerity, and straightforwardness we represent. We have never used cunning during these proceedings. Meanwhile, our opponents are too often cunning, and people sense this. Indeed, the truth has an ontological, existential superiority over deception, and this is even described in the Bible, particularly in the Old Testament. The paths of truth always triumph over the paths of cunning, guile, and deception. Every day, truth grows more victorious, despite the fact that we remain behind bars and will probably be here for a long time.

Yesterday, Madonna performed in Moscow with "Pussy Riot" written on her back. More and more people see that we are held here illegally and on false pretenses. This amazes me. I am amazed that truth really does triumph over deception. Despite the fact that we are physically here, we are freer than everyone sitting across from us on the side of the prosecution. We can say anything we want and we do say everything we want. The prosecution can only say what they are permitted to say by political censorship. They can't say "punk prayer," "Virgin Mary, Put Putin Away," they can't utter a single line of our punk prayer that deals with the political system.

Perhaps they think that it would be good to put us in prison because we speak out against Putin and his regime. They don't say so because they aren't allowed to. Their mouths are sewn shut. Unfortunately, they are only here as dummies. But I hope they realize this and ultimately pursue the path of freedom, truth, and sincerity, because this path is superior to the path of complete stagnation, false modesty, and hypocrisy. Stagnation and the search for truth are always at odds, and in this case, in the course of this trial, we see on the one side people who attempt to know the truth, and on the other side people who are trying to fetter those people.

A human being is a creature who is always in error, never perfect. She quests for wisdom, but cannot possess it; this is why philosophy was born. This is why the philosopher is the one who loves wisdom and yearns for it, but does not yet possess it. This is what ultimately calls a human being to action, to think and live in a certain way. It was our search for truth that led us to the Cathedral of Christ the Savior. I think that Christianity, as I understood it while studying the Old and especially the New Testament, supports the search for truth and a constant overcoming of oneself, the overcoming of what you were earlier. It was not in vain that when Christ was among the prostitutes, he said that those who falter should be helped: "I forgive them," he said. I do not see this spirit in our trial, which takes place under the banner of Christianity. Instead, it seems to me that the prosecution is trampling on religion.

The lawyers for the [official] "injured parties" are abandoning them—that is how I interpret it. Two days ago, [one of the lawyers of the injured parties] Alexei Taratukhin made a speech in which he insisted that under no circumstances should anyone assume that the lawyer agrees with the parties he represents. In other words, the lawyer finds himself in an ethically uncomfortable position and does not want to stand for the people who seek to imprison Pussy Riot. I don't know why they want to put us in prison. Maybe they have the right to, but I want to emphasize that their lawyer himself seems to be ashamed. Perhaps he was affected by the people shouting, "Executioners! Shame on you!" I want to point out that truth and goodness always triumph over deception and malice. It also seems to me that the prosecution attorneys are being influenced by some higher power, because time after time, they slip up and call us "the injured party." Almost all of the lawyers have accidentally said this, and even prosecution attorney Larisa Pavlova, who is very negatively disposed toward us, nonetheless appears to be moved by some higher power when she refers to us as "the injured party." She does not say this about those she represents, but only about us.

I don't want to label anyone. It seems to me that there are no winners, losers, victims, or defendants here. We all simply need to reach each other, connect, and establish a dialogue in order to seek out the truth together. Together, we can be philosophers and seek wisdom, instead of stigmatizing people and labeling them. That is the last thing a person should do. Christ condemned it. With this trial, the system is abusing us. Who would have thought that man and the state he rules could, again and again, perpetrate absolutely unmotivated evil? Who could have imagined that history, especially Stalin's still-recent Great Terror, could fail to teach us anything? The medieval Inquisition methods that reign in the law enforcement and judicial systems of our country, the Russian Federation, are enough to make you weep. But from the moment of our arrest, we have stopped weeping. We have lost our ability to cry. We shouted desperately at our punk concerts. With all our might, we decried the lawlessness of the authorities, the governing bodies. But now, our voices have been taken away. They were taken from us on March 3, 2012, when we were arrested. The following day, our voices and our votes were stolen from among the millions at the so-called elections.

During the entire trial, some people have refused to hear us. Hearing us would mean being receptive to what we are saying, to be thoughtful, to strive toward wisdom, to be philosophers. I believe that every person should aspire to this, and not only those who have studied in some philosophy department. A formal education means nothing, although prosecution attorney Pavlova attempts constantly to reproach us for our lack of education. We believe the most important thing is to strive toward knowledge and understanding. This is what a person can achieve independently, outside the walls of an educational institution. Regalia and advanced scholarly degrees mean nothing. A person can possess a great deal of knowledge, but not act as a human being. Pythagoras said that extensive knowledge does not breed wisdom. Unfortunately, we are here to affirm that. We are here only as decorations, inanimate elements, mere bodies that have been delivered into the courtroom. Our motions—after many days of requests, negotiations, and struggles—are given no consideration, they are always denied. Unfortunately for us and for our country, the court hears a prosecutor who constantly distorts our words and statements with impunity, neutering them. The foundational adversarial principle of the legal system is openly and demonstrably violated.

On July 30, the first day of the trial, we presented our reaction to the prosecutors' indictments. At that time, the court categorically refused us the right to speak, and our written texts were read aloud by our defense lawyer, Violetta Volkova. For us, this was the first opportunity we had to express ourselves after five months of incarceration. Until then we had been incarcerated, confined; we can't do anything from there, we can't write appeals, we can't film what is happening around us, we have no Internet, our lawyer can't even bring us papers because even that is forbidden. On July 30, we spoke openly for the first time; we called for making contact and facilitating dialogue, not for battle or confrontation. We reached our hands out to the people who, for some reason, consider us their enemies, and they spat into our open hands. "You are not sincere," they told us. Too bad. Do not judge us according to your own behavior. We spoke sincerely, as we always do. We said what we thought. We were unbelievably childlike, naive in our truth, but nonetheless we are not sorry for our words, and this includes our words on that day. And having been maligned ourselves, we do not want to malign others in response. We are in desperate circumstances, but we do not despair. We are persecuted, but we have not been abandoned. It is easy to degrade and destroy people who are so open, but "when I am weak, then I am strong."

Listen to our words and not to what [pro-Putin television journalist] Arkady Mamontov says about us. Do not distort and falsify what we say. Allow us to enter into a dialogue, into contact with this country, which is ours also, and not only the land of Putin and the patriarch. Just like Solzhenitsyn, I believe that in the end the word will break through the cement. Solzhenitsyn wrote, "Thus, the word is more essential than cement. Thus, the word is not a small nothing. In this manner, noble people begin to grow, and their word will break cement."

Katya, Masha, and I may be in prison, but I do not consider us defeated. Just as the dissidents were not defeated; although they disappeared into mental institutions and prisons, they still pronounced their verdict upon the regime. The art of creating the image of an epoch does not know any winners or losers. It was the same with the OBERIU poets, who remained artists until the end, inexplicable and incomprehensible. Purged in 1937, Alexander Vvedensky wrote, "The incomprehensible pleases us, the inexplicable is our friend." According to the official death certificate, Aleksandr Vvedensky died on December 20, 1941. No one knows the cause of death. It could have been dysentery on the train on the way to the camps; it could have been the bullet of a guard. It occurred somewhere on the railroad between Voronezh and Kazan.

Pussy Riot are Vvedensky's students and heirs. His principle of the bad rhyme is dear to us. He wrote, "Occasionally, I think of two different rhymes, a good one and a bad one, and I always choose the bad one because it is always the right one."

"The inexplicable is our friend": the highbrow and refined works of the OBERIU poets and their search for thought on the edge of meaning were finally embodied when they paid for their art with their lives, which were taken by the senseless and inexplicable Great Terror. Paying with their lives, these poets unintentionally proved that irrationality and senselessness were at the core of their era. Thus, the artistic became historical fact. The price of participation in the creation of history is immeasurably great for the individual. But the essence of human existence lies precisely in this participation. To be a beggar, and yet to enrich others. To have nothing, but to possess all. One considers the OBERIU dissidents dead, but they are alive. They are punished, but they do not die.

Do you remember why young Dostoyevsky was sentenced to death? His entire guilt lay in the fact that he was fascinated by socialist theories, and during meetings of freethinkers and friends—who met on Fridays in the apartment of [Mikhail] Petrashevsky—he discussed the writings of [Joseph] Fourier and George Sand. On one of the last Fridays, he read [Vissarion] Belinsky's letter to [Nikolai] Gogol aloud, a letter that was filled, according to the court that tried Dostoevsky (listen!), "with impudent statements against the Orthodox Church and the state government." After all the preparations for execution and "ten agonizing, infinitely terrifying minutes awaiting death" (Dostoyevsky), it was announced that the sentence was changed to four years of hard labor in Siberia, followed by military service.

Socrates was accused of corrupting youth with his philosophical discussions and refusing to accept the Athenian gods. He had a living connection with the divine voice, and he was not, as he insisted many times, by any account an enemy of the gods. But what did that matter when Socrates irritated the influential citizens of his city with his critical, dialectical thought, free of prejudice? Socrates was sentenced to death and, having refused to escape Athens (as his students proposed), he courageously emptied a cup of hemlock and died. Have you forgotten under what circumstances Stephen, the disciple of the Apostles, concluded his earthly life? "Then they secretly induced men to say, 'We have heard him speak blasphemous words against Moses and against God.' And they stirred up the people, the elders and the scribes, and they came up to him and dragged him away and brought him before the Council. They put forward false witnesses who said, 'This man incessantly speaks against this holy place and the Law.'" [Acts 6:11-13] He was found guilty and stoned to death. I also hope that you all remember well how the Jews answered Christ: "It is not for good works that we are going to stone you but for blasphemy." [John 10:33] And finally we would do well to keep in mind the following characterization of Christ: "He is demon-possessed and raving mad." [John 10:20]

If the authorities, tsars, presidents, prime ministers, the people, and judges understood what "I desire mercy, not sacrifice" [Matthew 9:13] meant, they would not put the innocent on trial. Our authorities, however, still rush to us with condemnations, and never reprieves. To this point, I would like to thank Dmitri Anatolyevich Medvedev for providing us with the following excellent aphorism. He summarized his presidential term with the statement: "Liberty is better than non-liberty." Thus in line with Medvedev's apt words, Putin's third term can well be characterized by the aphorism, "Prison is better than stoning." I ask that you consider carefully the following from Montaigne's *Essays*, which were written in the sixteenth century, preaching tolerance and the skeptical rejection of any unilateral system or doctrine: "It is putting a very high value on one's conjectures, to have a man roasted alive because of them."

Is it worth it to pass judgment on people and put them in prison based on conjectures not substantiated by the prosecution? Since we truly have never harbored any religious hatred or animosity, our accusers have to rely on false witnesses. One of them, Matilda Ivashchenko, became ashamed of herself and did not appear in court. Then there were the false testimonies of Mr. Troitsky and Mr. Ponkin, as well as Mrs. Abramenkova. There is no proof of our hatred and animosity except for the so-called "expert evaluation," which the court, if it is honest and fair, must consider unacceptable as factual proof, as it is not a rigorous and objective text, but a dirty and false little paper reminiscent of the Inquisition. There is no other evidence that can confirm the existence of such a motive. The prosecutors have refused to voice excerpts from Pussy Riot interviews, since these excerpts would only further prove the absence of any motive. Why wasn't the following text by us—which, incidentally, appeared in the affidavit—presented by the prosecution? "We respect religion in general and the Orthodox faith in particular. This is why we are especially infuriated when Christian philosophy, which is full of light, is used in such a dirty fashion. It makes us sick to see such beautiful ideas forced to their knees." This quote appeared in an interview that the *Russian Reporter* conducted with Pussy Riot the day after our performance. We still feel sick, and it causes us real pain to look at all this. Finally, the lack of any hatred or animosity toward religion and the religious is affirmed by all character witnesses called in to testify by our lawyers.

Apart from all these character references, I ask you to consider the results of the psychological and psychiatric evaluations in Detention Center Number 6, ordered by the prison authorities. The report revealed the following: the values that I embrace are justice, mutual respect, humaneness, equality, and freedom. This was written by a court expert, a person who does not know me personally, though it is possible that Ranchenko, the interrogator, desired a different conclusion. But it seems that there are more people in our world who love and value truth than those who don't. The Bible is correct about this.

In conclusion, I would like to read the words of a Pussy Riot song that, strange as it may be, proved prophetic. We foresaw that "the Head of the KGB and the Chief Saint of the land place the protesters under guard and take them to prison." This was about us. Neither myself, nor Alyokhina, nor Samutsevich were found to have powerful and stable affects, or other psychological values, that could be interpreted as hatred toward anything or anyone.

So:

Open all the doors, tear off your epaulettes
Come, taste freedom with us.

Closing Courtroom Statement by Masha

This trial is highly typical and speaks volumes. The current government will have occasion to feel shame and embarrassment because of it for a long time to come. At each stage it has embodied a travesty of justice. As it turned out, our performance, at first a small and somewhat absurd act, snowballed into an enormous catastrophe. This would obviously not happen in a healthy society. Russia, as a state, has long resembled an organism that is sick to the core. And the sickness explodes out into the open when you rub up against its inflamed abscesses. At first, and for a long time, this sickness gets hushed in public, but eventually it always finds resolution through dialogue. And look—this is the kind of dialogue that our government is capable of. This trial is not only a malignant and grotesque mask, it is the face of the government's dialogue with the people of our country. To prompt discussion about a problem on the societal level, you often need the right conditions—an impetus.

And it is interesting that our situation was depersonalized from the start. This is because when we talk about Putin, we have in mind first and foremost not Vladimir Vladimirovich Putin, but Putin the System that he himself created—the vertical power, where all control is carried out effectively by one person. And that vertical power is uninterested, completely uninterested in the opinion of the masses. And what worries me most of all is that the opinion of the younger generations is not taken into consideration. We believe that the ineffectiveness of this administration is evident in practically everything.

And right here, in this closing statement, I would like to describe my firsthand experience of running afoul of this system. Our schooling, which is where the personality begins to form in a social context, effectively ignores any particularities of the individual. There is no individual approach, no study of culture, philosophy, or basic knowledge about civic society. Officially, these subjects do exist, but they are still taught according to the Soviet model. And as a result, we see the marginalization of contemporary art in the public consciousness, a lack of motivation for philosophical thought, and gender stereotyping. The concept of the human being as a citizen gets swept away into a distant corner.

Today's educational institutions teach people, from childhood, to live as automatons, and not to pose the crucial questions consistent with their age. They inculcate cruelty and intolerance of nonconformity. Beginning in childhood, we forget our freedom.

I have personal experience with psychiatric clinics for minors. And I can say with conviction that any teenager who shows any signs of active nonconformity can end up in such a place. A certain percentage of the kids there are from orphanages. In our country, it's considered entirely normal to commit a child to a psychiatric clinic who has tried to escape from an orphanage. And they treat them using extremely powerful sedatives like Aminazin, which was also used to subdue Soviet dissidents in the 1970s.

This experience is especially traumatizing given the overall punitive tendency of the environment and the absence of any real psychological assistance. All interactions are based on exploiting children's feelings of fear and forcing them into submission. And as a result, their own cruelty increases many times over. Many children there are illiterate, but no one makes any effort to battle this—to the contrary, every last drop of motivation for personal development is discouraged. The individual closes off entirely and loses faith in the world.

I would like to note that this method of personal development clearly impedes the awakening of both inner freedoms and religious freedoms, unfortunately, on a mass scale. The consequence of the process I have just described is ontological humility, existential humility, and socialization. To me, this transition, or rupture, is noteworthy in that, if approached from the point of view of Christian culture, we see that meanings and symbols are being replaced by those that are diametrically opposed to them. Thus one of the most important Christian concepts, humility, is now commonly understood not as a path toward perception, fortification, and ultimate liberation, but on the contrary, as an instrument for enslavement. To quote [Russian philosopher] Nikolai Berdyaev, one could say that "the ontology of humility is the ontology of the slaves of God, and not the sons of God." When I was involved with organizing the ecological movement, I became fundamentally convinced of the priority of inner freedom as the foundation for taking action, as well as the importance, the direct importance, of taking action as such.

To this day I find it astonishing that, in our country, we need the support of several thousands of individuals in order to put an end to the despotism of one or a handful of bureaucrats. I would like to note that our trial stands as a very eloquent confirmation of the fact that we need the support of thousands of individuals from all over the world in order to prove the obvious: the three of us are not guilty. We are not guilty; the whole world says so. The whole world says it at concerts, the whole world says it on the Internet, the whole world says it in the press. They say it in parliament. The prime minister of England greets our president not with words about the Olympics, but with the question, "Why are three innocent women sitting in prison?" It's shameful.

But I find it even more astonishing that people don't believe that they can have any influence on the regime. During the pickets and demonstrations [of the winter and spring], back when I was collecting signatures and organizing petitions, many people would ask me—and ask me with sincere bewilderment—why in the world they should care about, or what business they could possibly have with, that little patch of forest in the Krasnodar region–even though it is perhaps unique in Russia, perhaps primeval? Why should they care if the wife of our Prime Minister Dmitri Medvedev wants to build an official residence there and destroy the only juniper preserve in Russia? This is yet another confirmation that people in our country have lost the sense that this country belongs to us, its citizens. They no longer have a sense of themselves as citizens. They have a sense of themselves simply as automated masses. They don't feel that the forest belongs to them, even when the forest is located right next to their own houses. I doubt they even feel a sense of ownership over their own homes. Because if someone were to drive up to their porches with a bulldozers and tell them that they need to evacuate—"Excuse us, we're going raze your house to make room for a bureaucrat's residence"—these people would obediently collect their belongings and go out on the street. And then they would stay there precisely until the regime tells them what they should do next. They are completely helpless, it is very sad. Having spent almost half a year in jail, I have come to understand that prison is just Russia in miniature.

One could also begin with the system of governance. This is that very same vertical power, in which every decision takes place solely through the direct intervention of the man in charge. There is absolutely no horizontal delegation of duties, which would make everyone's lives noticeably easier. And there is a lack of individual initiative. Denunciation thrives along with mutual suspicion. In jail, as in our country as a whole, everything is designed to strip people of their individuality, to identify a person only with a function, whether that function is as a worker or as a prisoner. The strict framework of the daily schedule in prison (you get used to it quickly) resembles the framework of daily life that everyone is born into.

In this framework, people begin to place high value on meaningless trifles. In prison these trifles are things like a tablecloth or plastic dishes that can only be procured with the personal permission of the head warden. Outside prison, accordingly, you have social status, which people also value a great deal. This has always been surprising to me. Another element of this framework is becoming aware of how this government functions as a performance, a play. While in reality, it turns into chaos. The surface-level organization of the regime falls away to reveal the disorganization and inefficiency of most of its activities. And it's obvious that this doesn't lead to any real governance. On the contrary, people start to feel an ever-stronger sense of being lost—including being lost even in time and space. In jail and all over the country, people don't know where to turn with this or that question. That's why they turn to the boss of the jail. And outside the prison, correspondingly, the people go to Putin, the top boss.

Expressing in a text a collective image of the system that . . . well, in general, I could say that we aren't against . . . that we are against the Putin-engendered chaos, which can only superficially be called a government. Expressing a collective image of the system, in which, in our opinion, practically all the institutions are undergoing a kind of mutation, while still appearing nominally intact. And in which the civil society so dear to us is being destroyed. We are not making direct quotations in our texts; we only take the form of a direct quotation as an artistic formula. The only thing that's the same is our motivation. Our motivation is the same motivation that goes with the use of a direct quotation. This motivation is best expressed in the Gospels: "For everyone who asks receives; the one who seeks finds; and to the one who knocks, the door will be opened." [Matthew 7:8] I—all of us—sincerely believe that for us the door will be opened. But alas, for now the only thing that has happened is that we've been locked up in prison. It is very strange that in their reaction to our actions, the authorities completely disregard the historical experience of dissent. "[H]ow unfortunate is the country where simple honesty is understood, in the best case, as heroism. And in the worst case as a mental disorder," the dissident [Vladimir] Bukovsky wrote in the 1970s. And even though it hasn't been very long, now people are acting as if there was never any Great Terror nor any attempts to resist it. I believe that we are being accused by people without memory. Many of them have said, "He is possessed by a demon and insane. Why do you listen to Him?" These words belong to the Jews who accused Jesus Christ of blasphemy. They said, "We are . . . stoning you . . . for blasphemy." [John 10:33] Interestingly enough, it is precisely this verse that the Russian Orthodox Church uses to express its opinion about blasphemy.

This view is certified on paper; it's attached to our criminal file. Expressing this opinion, the Russian Orthodox Church refers to the Gospels as static religious truth. The Gospels are no longer understood as revelation, which they have been since the very beginning, but rather as a monolithic chunk that can be disassembled into quotations to be shoved in wherever necessary—in any of its documents, for any of their purposes. The Russian Orthodox Church did not even bother to look up the context in which "blasphemy" is mentioned here—that in this case, the word applies to Jesus Christ himself. I think that religious truth should not be static, that it is essential to understand the instances and paths of spiritual development, the trials of a human being, his duplicity, his splintering. That for one's self to form it is essential to experience these things. That you have to experience all these things in order to develop as a person. That religious truth is a process and not a finished product that can be shoved wherever and whenever.

And all of these things I've been talking about, all of these processes—they acquire meaning in art and in philosophy, including contemporary art. An artistic situation can, and in my opinion, must contain its own internal conflict. And what really irritates me is how the prosecution uses the words "so-called" in reference to contemporary art.

I would like to point out that very similar methods were used during the trial of [Joseph] Brodsky. His poems were defined as "so-called" poems; the witnesses for the prosecution hadn't actually read them—just as a number of the witnesses in our case didn't see the performance itself and only watched the clip online. Our apologies, it seems, are also being defined by the collective prosecuting body as "so-called" apologies. This is offensive. And I am overwhelmed with moral injury and psychological trauma. Because our apologies were sincere. I am sorry that so many words have been uttered and you all still haven't understood this. Or it is calculated deviousness when you say our apologies are insincere. I don't know what you still need to hear from us. But for me this trial is a "so-called" trial. And I am not afraid of you. I am not afraid of falsehood and fictitiousness, of sloppily disguised deception, in the verdict of the "so-called" court.

Because all you can deprive me of is "so-called" freedom. This is the only kind that exists in Russia. But nobody can take away my inner freedom. It lives in the word, it will go on living thanks to openness [*glasnost*], when this will be read and heard by thousands of people. This freedom goes on living with every person who is not indifferent, who hears us in this country. With everyone who found shards of themselves in the trial, like in previous times when they found them in Franz Kafka and Guy Debord. I have honesty and openness, I thirst for the truth; and these things will make all of us just a little bit more free. We will see this one day.

Three Poems by Masha

WHAT FOLLOWS FEAR

Oh, what are we?
Fear is what follows in conclusion.
And what does it make us?
After we'd smashed into drops, into walls
Whose eyes found us?
Just yours, good God, yours alone.
Guide my hand
When I throw a fistful of words
and I betray you right away
Wait for me. On the seashore
On the quay
I will escape them
I will run away

IN LIGHT OF CURRENT EVENTS

Bad things aren't scary to do; everyone does them.
It's not hard to hide in a crowd, no one will notice.
One piece of trash more, one piece less.
What's there to be said—it's the times we live in,
    they're like that.
We got unlucky. But, no.
You cannot be afraid or ashamed to do good.
You cannot.
There's so frighteningly little of that around these days.
Cynicism's in fashion.
Ironic smiles and dull melancholy.
Know this: if you don't do it, possibly, no one will.
A lot of them just don't have the time to look at
    what they're doing, let alone the time to take stock.
They have time to look at others, they have time
    to assign blame.
If you choose to do good, if you choose to help
    come what may, know this: you have lost.
You have most certainly lost.

But this doesn't mean that you mustn't do it.

It is important to remember who we are.

It is important to know that your conscience is what matters.

It is important to follow your conscience.

It is important not so much to change things, but to know that you are changing them.

IN SNOWS OVER BRIDGES

I change into things:
I hang like a convict
I'm dining with kings.
My broken-down carriage
Careens down your street
And under the snow
I'll lie down for a bit.
I'm dining with freaks,
I change as I go,
I stand like a king
Under bridges in snow.
When my child sleeps, the night,
Time altogether, seems to stop, and turn to water,
Into a sea that unites all with all; even, possibly,
Me with you.
And the greatest treasure would be safe in it,
Afloat on a simple raft. I'll attach every tree to a place
Where people will find it, recognize it and remember.

They say that home is where you are always missed.
When I hear things like this
I feel like twisting the speaker's neck
Into a tight tourniquet, and then, steadily,
Making him look
At the rocking of the baby's cradle.
Then I want to take his hand and say: see
How the lilac's blooming, can you feel the scent?
Not a thing will be left of us, but this will go on.
Will go on.

Excerpts from the Appeal Statements

We are not guilty. I think this is obvious. I also think that our court sentence should be declared invalid. Dear believers, we did not want to insult you. We have never had such intentions. We went to the cathedral to voice our protest against the merging of religious elites with the political elites of our country. . . . We have been jailed for our political beliefs. Even if we are sent to Siberia we will not be silent.

—Masha

It's painful for me to hear that I am speaking out against religion. I have no religious hatred and never have. I want to warn that everything that is happening in Putin's third term is leading to the end of stability. In two years there will be civil war, because Putin is doing everything to ensure that. . . . We'll be going to a prison colony while civil war is brewing in this country. Putin is doing everything to make this happen. He is setting people against each other.

—Nadya

If we unwillingly hurt any of believers by our actions, then we apologize for that. The idea of our action was political, not religious. In our previous actions, as in this one too, we have been protesting against the power of the current president, against the merging of the church with state authorities, and against political statements by the patriarch. Therefore I believe I have not committed a crime. This is the joint position of all three of us. There is no split within Pussy Riot.

—Katya

TRIBUTES TO PUSSY RIOT

Yoko Ono

Dear Yekaterina Samutsevich [Katya],
    Thank you. You are right. You have won!
You have won for all of us, the women of the world.
The power of your every word is now growing in us.
From here on, please take good care of yourself, as much as you are allowed to.
Each one of us is very much needed now.
Let's cleanse ourselves for the next battle, and heal the world with the power of truth.
War Is Over! (If You Want It.)
In sisterhood,

Yoko Ono *is an artist, writer, musician, and peace activist.*

Free Pussy Riot!

Peaches and Simonne Jones

Free Pussy Riot
Free Pussy Riot
Free Pussy, try it
Free Pussy Riot

Church and state separate
Shoot a flare for the punk prayer
Screw your old school papa greed
Anarchist feminist what we need

Free Pussy Riot
Free Pussy Riot
Free Pussy, try it
Free Pussy Riot

Maria Alyokhina
Yekaterina Samutsevich
Nadezhda Tolokonnikova

I love you I don't care
I love you it's not fair

I love you anarchy
Set us free set us free

Here's the pitch
Here's the switch
Put Putin on a stick and play burn the witch
So poor so rich
Seven year itch
Putin Pussy Riot run this shit

A bitch is a bitch is a bitch is a bitch is a bitch is a bitch
Patriarchal bullshit
A bitch is a bitch is a bitch is a bitch is a bitch is a bitch
Patriarchal bullshit

I love you I don't care
I love you it's not fair

Set us free set us free

Free Pussy Riot

Free Pussy Riot
Free Pussy, try it
Free Pussy Riot

Free Pussy Riot
Free Pussy Riot
Free Pussy, try it
Free Pussy Riot

We are all Pussy Riot We are all Pussy Riot We are all Pussy
Riot We are all Pussy Riot We are all Pussy Riot We are all
Pussy Riot We are all Pussy Riot

Peaches *is a musician and performer. Her LPs include* The
Teaches from Peaches, Impeach My Bush, *and* I Feel Cream.
Simonne Jones *is a multi-instrumentalist and visual artist.*

On Pussy Riot: A Punk Prayer for Freedom

Bianca Jagger

If the freedom of speech is taken away then dumb and silent we may be led, like sheep to the slaughter. —*George Washington*

Yekaterina Samutsevich, Maria Alyokhina, and Nadezhda Tolokonnikova, the three brave members of Pussy Riot, are not ready to be led like sheep to the slaughter. They have stood up in defense of free speech and human rights in Russia. Amnesty International has designated Pussy Riot prisoners of conscience, "wrongfully prosecuted and convicted solely for the peaceful expression of their beliefs." It's vital that we stand with them, and use all possible means to raise awareness of this miscarriage of justice.

The release of Yekaterina Samutsevich on a probationary suspended sentence on October, 10, 2012, is not enough. Maria Alyokhina and Nadezhda Tolokonnikova were condemned in October 2012 to serve the remainder of their terms, which end in March 2014, in a remote penal colony. None of these women should have been prosecuted, and none should languish in prison. Their arrests and detention are a flagrant human rights violation reminiscent of the dark days of the Soviet Union. The persecution of Pussy Riot has no place in a democratic Russia. The imprisonment of Pussy Riot has troubling implications for artistic and intellectual freedom in Russia. It suggests the country is moving toward a point where those who express opposition to government policy could be prosecuted. As former Russian Finance Minister Alexey Kudrin said, "The verdict in the case against the Pussy Riot punk band isn't only a fact in the lives of three young women; it is also yet another blow to the justice system and, above all, Russian citizens' belief in it."*

In September 2012 I spoke at an event in New York, with Pyotr Verzilov, husband of Nadezhda Tolokonnikova. I am very concerned for their daughter Gera, who was also there. For a period of six months, Gera was not allowed to see her mother. Now, with Nadezhda nearly one thousand miles away from Moscow, in a camp in Perm, an area notorious for housing the harshest of Russia's prison camps, Gera will see her mother even less.

It is inspiring to see the support that has gathered behind Pussy Riot. Their plight has sparked protests all over the world. In 2012 they were nominated for the prestigious Sakharov Prize for Freedom of Thought.

Throughout history countless artists have denounced the abuses of their time. They have stood up for democratic principles, the rule of law, freedom of speech, and civil liberties. Many of these courageous artists have also been persecuted, and incarcerated.

Tibetan filmmaker Dhondup Wangchen is under arrest in the Peoples' Republic of China, for criticizing the Chinese government in his documentary, *Leaving Fear Behind*, in which he

*http://www.guardian.co.uk/world/2012/aug/18/pussy-riot-russia-global-protest

interviewed ordinary Tibetan people on their views of the Dalai Lama and the Chinese government in the run up to the Beijing Olympics. Like Pussy Riot, Dhondup Wangchen has been designated a prisoner of conscience by Amnesty International.

Renowned Chinese artist Ai Weiwei's outspoken criticism of the Chinese government led to his arrest in 2011. He was detained by police in solitary confinement at a secret location for eighty-one days. He is currently being held under arbitrary bail conditions in Beijing.

In 2010 filmmaker Jafar Panahi was sentenced to six years in prison in Iran for "propaganda against the state." He was banned for an additional twenty years from artistic activities, including filmmaking, writing scripts, travelling abroad, and speaking with the media. He is currently under house arrest, and could be forced to report for prison at any time. His latest film, *This Is Not a Film*, was smuggled out of Iran in a cake.

Painter Owen Maseko is awaiting trial in Zimbabwe, for his 2010 exhibition of paintings depicting the massacres of Ndebele civilians during the Gukurahundi in the 1980s. He was charged with "undermining the authority" of President Robert Mugabe.

The Bianca Jagger Human Rights Foundation, of which I am founder and chair, supports the fundamental right to freedom of expression without fear of imprisonment or reprisals.

I call for the immediate and unconditional release of Maria Alyokhina and Nadezhda Tolokonnikova, and the lifting of Yekaterina Samutsevich's suspended sentence. I urge everyone who reads this book to sign Amnesty International's petition to Yuri Yakovlevich Chaika, Prosecutor General, and Sergey I. Kislyak, Russian Ambassador to the US. We have all seen the power of social media. Let's use that power to take to Twitter, Facebook, Google, Google+, LinkedIn, and other social networking sites: in support of Pussy Riot, in support of artists who are prisoners of conscience, who are persecuted for their art and beliefs.

As the poet John Milton said, who was forced into hiding for his political beliefs: "Give me the liberty to know, to utter, and to argue freely according to conscience, above all liberties."

Bianca Jagger is the founder and chair of the Bianca Jagger Human Rights Foundation.

Punk as Protest: Join the Party

Tobi Vail

Pussy Riot's punk is pure protest. They don't need a publicist or a record label or a booking agent. Nothing is for sale.

Pussy Riot is a non-commercial venture. They play unsanctioned shows exclusively—they don't play rock clubs, they don't tour. They exist outside of commodity exchange. They are not a part of the entertainment-industrial complex. They are on a heroic mission to speak truth to power.

Pussy Riot doesn't need the radio. Their music is the soundtrack of radical feminist action. Video footage shows them seizing control of territory that doesn't belong to them— the roof of a detention center, the subway, a fashion boutique, Red Square, the biggest cathedral in Moscow—obliterating the line between private property and public space. Upon taking over, they perform their songs on the world stage.

Before Pussy Riot members were jailed, they were confident that the struggle would continue: "We have nothing to worry about, because if the repressive Putinist police crooks throw one of us in prison, five, ten, fifteen more girls will put on colorful balaclavas and continue the fight against their symbols of power."

Pussy Riot started in Moscow but chapters are forming all

over the world in response to group members' unjust imprisonment and continued state harassment. In the age of the archive, Pussy Riot propels punk into the twenty-first century, presenting a new model for the creation of a culture of protest outside of capitalism.

Put on a balaclava, pick up a guitar, and hit the streets. Take over a government building, a defense plant, a shopping mall, and make your voice heard. Document your action to participate in the conversation and show your solidarity with Nadezhda, Yekaterina, and Maria. We are all Pussy Riot.

Tobi Vail is an Olympia-based writer and musician best known for her work in Bikini Kill and Jigsaw. She currently plays in three underground bands, volunteers at the public library, and does mail order for Bikini Kill Records (bikinikill.com). You can keep up with her cultural work via jigsawunderground.blogspot.com and twitter.com/mstobivail.

Johanna Fateman

As the women of Pussy Riot have breathtakingly commandeered the international spotlight with their brightly colored outfits and balaclavas, they've also given us the gift of their writings. I'm so moved by their radical bewilderment of their missives. The imprisoned artists are scholars of Putinist repression; they *know*, but they are still shocked by its violent reprisals, hypocrisy, corruption, and woman hating. They can be brilliantly sardonic too. But what brings me to tears is their outraged wonder at the regime that wants them jaded and servile, that has locked them up, and that has famously shamed itself in doing so.

Johanna Fateman is a writer, musician, producer, and member of the feminist electropunk band Le Tigre.

JD Samson

Part of what pushed me to start working for Pussy Riot's release is that I know they would do the same for me. We are all part of the punk feminist activist art community, and to me that means standing by my sisters and creating visibility for their case. At this point, we must be a channel for their incredible voices. They may be in prison, but Pussy Riot is winning. In a statement written by Nadya the day before the verdict, she agrees. "I am grateful to everyone who said: 'Free Pussy Riot!' We are all making history—an important political event—and Putin's system will find it harder and harder to control us. Whatever Pussy Riot's verdict is, we are already winning. This is because we have learned how to be politically angry and vocal."

This revolution is a window into the Russian political system. As feminists we are shocked to see that in Russia the word "feminism" is blasphemous. As Americans we may be shocked to see absolutely no separation of church and state. But we also know that's the reality in the US as well. So we must stand up, because this is not only a window into Russia, but also a window into our own government and our own fight for personal freedoms.

JD Samson *is a musician, DJ, member of the feminist electropunk band Le Tigre, and leads Brooklyn-based band and art/ performance collective MEN.*

Eileen Myles

Dear Pussy Riot,
 I'm a fan and co-conspirator in regards to all the meanings of your performance, which has created so much important turmoil in Russia and in the world. I realized the other day that the one piece of what you've done that feels most important to me is the strange and beautiful fact that your action supported a woman's right to pray. I've been reading about money and male power lately and how important it is that men are on coins and paper money—and sometimes there are two men—but women are rarely on money. Some of the meaning of men's presence on money is that it represents an imperial prayer between father and son. That is what governments and history and religion and ideology are based on—men's imperial prayer, which will always be uttered both publicly and privately, and that power will be passed from father to son and everyone will witness that display and worship in all the palaces of power, especially the church. When you asserted in your letter to the patriarch the sincerity of your prayer, I wondered for a moment if you were being ingenuous. But the more I've thought about it, after reading the court documents, I've realized what prayer is and was and that female prayers are kept hidden so there will be no spectacle of

female power in the world. All our actions must be hidden in order to support this grander force, which is generally male, be he the president, the father, the patriarch, or the police. You prayed publicly in a church, and the cat is out of the bag now. The world has heard you, and your tumultuous prayer will never be taken back.

Eileen Myles is an award winning poet and author of many books including Inferno. *She is a Professor Emeritus of Writing at UC San Diego and lives in New York.*

Mx Justin Vivian Bond

The fierce intelligence, conviction, and courage of Pussy Riot in the face of outrageous patriarchal tomfoolery makes them role models and guiding lights leading the way toward a future aspired to by an overwhelming percentage of people of all genders throughout the world.

Thank you, Pussy Riot, for opening our eyes to the power and possibility we each hold within us as vulnerable individuals, artists, and marginalized communities, and thank you for exposing the crumbling bulwark of the entrenched, the vicious, and the ignorant power mongers within the oppressive state and religious hierarchies worldwide. Blessings.

Justin Vivian Bond is a singer-songwriter and performance artist. Justin has released two solo albums, Dendrophile *and* Silver Wells, *and is the author of the award-winning memoir* Tango: My Childhood, Backwards and in High Heels.

Eyeholes and Mouthholes

Barbara Browning

I write this on October 10, 2012, shortly after the ruling on the appeal of Pussy Riot. At today's hearing, the sentence of Yekaterina Samutsevich was suspended, while those of Nadezhda Tolokonnikova and Maria Alyokhina were upheld. But this is, of course, an ongoing story, and it will continue to go on, whatever the legal developments—suspensions, upholdings, sentences served. Every point delivered in Samutsevich, Tolokonnikova, and Alyokhina's closing statements at the trial introduced, in fact, an opening: gashes in a mask—eyeholes ripped open for seeing clearly, a mouthhole for speaking truth.

Once you rip these holes open, there's no going back.

The figure of gashes in a mask evokes, of course, the balaclavas of Pussy Riot's performances. But the balaclavas are in fact there to draw your attention to a mask of another kind. In her closing statement at the trial, Alyokhina pointed out that it was the juridical process itself that was "a malignant and grotesque mask . . . the face of the government's dialogue with the people of our country." Pussy Riot's balaclavas aren't hiding anything. Instead, they reveal the ways that a repressive state masked its actions behind both religious and juridical institutions. Like the mask of the Zapatistas, Pussy Riot's balaclavas don't function to obscure the identity of the one, but to reveal the identity of a multitude. And while they join the Zapatistas in uncovering the insidious disguises of state oppression and capitalist manipulation, they do it with a difference: there's no mistaking that they're women.

Pussy Riot's unrelenting feminism—their real intervention—lies in their insistence that we understand the complicity not only of political oppression and of capitalism, but also of the patriarchy. Time to open up some eyeholes, and some mouthholes.

Barbara Browning is the author of the novels The Correspondence Artist *(winner of Lambda and Independent Press Book Awards) and* I'm Trying to Reach You. *She teaches in the Department of Performance Studies at NYU.*

Scrutinizing Girl Revolution Style Now

Vivien Goldman

Nobody can trust anybody now. I try not to go to protests," says Bullet, one of the ten or so members of the collective known as Pussy Riot. Part of the Russian avant-garde, the punk band is essentially just one persona of Pussy Riot's multiheaded goddess of a group: maybe Hydra, maybe Kali. Pussy Riot put a youthful female face on protest for those to whom "keeping it real" means still going to the hairdressers back in the old neighborhood.

Call it brave, call it blasphemy, but the trial against Pussy Riot has thrust what America's Riot Grrrls called "Revolution, Girl Style" into the spotlight. After five months in jail, Nadezhda Tolokonnikova, twenty-two, Maria Alyokhina, twenty-four, and Yekaterina Samutsevich, twenty-nine, face seven years in jail on hooliganism charges for performing "Punk Prayer," an anti-Putin song, in a cathedral. The vehemence of Putin's reaction suggests he's prepared to crush Pussy Riot's critique of the interdependence of the state and the Russian Orthodox Church, with their attack on women's reproductive control. Having caused a bigger controversy outside Russia than any oil oligarch, these agit-prop performance artists are both efficient and productive. And that's partly because Pussy Riot understand that to really express their ideas, there must also be a "Girl, Style Revolution."

Being a collective, their roles are fluid; but Pussy Rioter Bullet bravely agrees to Skype with me, anonymously. Camera off. During our interview, she comes up with her *nom de Pussy Riot*, Bullet. She feels it's a good fit. For a regular rock band, a stylist is there to make sure the musicians look good, according to conventional Western fashion norms. Bullet's job is rather different. "Pussy Riot use different codes of beauty, opposite to the traditional feminine image, in Russia or anywhere. Our look is not meant to be about long legs and high heels. The point is to be more surreal and Dada," explains Bullet. "This project is not about being good-looking; it's about being simple and strong.'"

Pussy Riot's style is simple to reproduce. You can be your own Pussy Riot stylistic supporter by improvising with what's around you. Clearly, whatever they may lack, they have access to an abundance of colorful, simple A-line and shift dresses in Russia. Bullet cheerfully advises us to steal from smart boutiques if you can't find what you want in thrift shops, flea markets, or in a friend's closet.

Bold, graphic color is their look's essential element. Prints and frou-frou are to be used only where necessary; and can often be roughly customized with scissors.

Though Pussy Riot eschew brands, the appeal of venerable British Doc Martens boots—the kicker of choice for punks and skinheads—is undeniable and well-founded. Even Pussy Riot cannot resist their practicality (coupled, these days, with whimsy.) However, some claim that genuine Doc Martens are too heavy to really run fast in—an essential element of Pussy

Riot style. Bedsides, true Doc Martens are costly. Bullet swears by tracking down working men's boots in small sizes instead.

At a Pussy Riot styling session, frocks obtained by any means possible are thrown in a heap on the floor to be swapped. The thing here is to make sure no Pussy Rioter wears the same ensemble twice (nothing to pin down the moving target of a Pussy Rioter). Their post-couture jumble aesthetic is influenced by the great trade winds. Much of their gaudy wardrobe is Made In China. The bright tights are the kind that are hard to find outside kid's sizes in New York, a fact that leaves Bullet gasping, but Bullet insists they stretch to fit an adult. Of course, the Pussy Rioters are all pretty skinny.

In true worker-bee fashion, the significance of the group way outweighs the perceived aesthetic "perfection" of any one individual. "That's why our balaclavas are so meaningful—it's not important to have a beautiful face," explains Bullet.

Artists like Bikini Kill, Kathleen Hanna, Rage Against the Machine, and Faith No More, along with demonstrators round the world, have been fashioning their own masks, fancier than Pussy Riot's (though they do fit each one by hand-stitching round the holes.) The customized balaclavas have been widely adopted as a symbol, and show that whatever our cause may be, in a sense We Are All Pussy Girls—if we only had the nerve.

The eyes, nose, and mouth holes of a basic balaclava are cut out of a regular woolen beanie hat unfolded to its full length. Much as Russia abounds in cheap Chinese imports, they appear to have more balaclava colors than anywhere in New York (again, to Bullet's surprise.)

Color is the subject of much heated philosophical debate among the Pussy Riot posse. "It is a miserable thing to talk sometimes, but for us it is a good thing to discuss," says Bullet. Anyone who has ever been in a collective or consciousness-raising group will relate. Is it possible to compare yellow and blue, they wonder? Black is banned, specifically from those crucial balaclavas, for its association with terrorists. Like free jazz musicians in search of the elusive note from a scale as yet unplumbed, Pussy Riot argue about the color with no name, and what that omni-color is, or might be, which is the essence of all colors—while being no known color at all. The meaning of true beauty is another popular topic. "You can be beautiful—or not so much," explains Bullet. Inverting the rock-biz-personality-cult norm, their aim is to conceal their identities, not promote them. Bullet is at pains to point out that they do not endorse those self-styled feminist punk bands whose visuals verge on softcore. "Without a bra, they look like photo models," she observes with some severity. "Pussy Riot is different."

Indeed, a Pussy Riot performance is different each time. They decide on a location and simply hit it, in and out, with a YouTube video of the event as record of its fleeting frenzy. The art attacks they have flashed in different public places—a chic shopping street, an art gallery, Red Square—never received as harsh a reaction as when they performed for mere seconds in the cathedral; they clearly hit a major nerve with the church and state axis.

For maximum impact in a very short time, often in adverse lighting conditions, a clever style strategy of Pussy Riot's is the use of simple graphic shapes in near-primary colors. Counterpointed by contrasting tights, the sizzling hues of their frocks pop against the gilt of the cathedral, or the reflective snow and glass surfaces of the high fashion shopping district they invaded—the favored couture haunt of top-ranking government dames. Wherever they strike, the anonymous girls are vivid and agile, their moves athletic and far removed from the regular wind 'n' grind video dance tropes.

Pussy Riot see themselves in a tradition of protest art. With the girls' bold, triumphant body language, stills of their "art pranks" recall triumphant proletarian workers on a poster by constructivist artist, Aleksandr Rodchenko (his artist wife, Varvara Stepanova, is an influence). The band do not work alone. The Voina (War) guerilla art movement, who advocate dumpster-diving in their off-the-grid approach, are key Pussy Riot associates.

Though they are best known as a band, Pussy Riot's music is rarely discussed. It is vigorous melodic punk, with choruses that ring like folk music. Their urgency energizes. "Our content is very poetic and rude," Bullet declares. "Pussy Riot songs are like leaflets; they must be short and well distributed and deal with a problem. Some feminists in Russia tried to analyze the text and found some controversial things that do not fit their concept of feminism," Bullet continues. "But it's silly, because when you analyze the Sex Pistols, they're not following the party line."

Perhaps most importantly, Bullet advises, "Pussy Riot is a good project to use to discuss different positions."

Vivien Goldman is a writer, broadcaster, educator, and post-punk musician. She teaches courses on punk and reggae at NYU, and is the author of five books, including The Book of Exodus: The Making and Meaning of Bob Marley and the Wailers' Album of the Century.

Laurie Weeks

Dear Pussy Riot,
        When I first heard the term Pussy Riot I laughed out
loud instantly. The hilarity remains undiminished. Pussy Riot
is the gift that keeps on giving, so thank you thank you thank
you. Virtually no comedy stone is left unturned in that combo
of terms, starting with the immediate full-body hit of delicious
juvenile stoner ridiculousity, which itself is a wave of deeply
serious intent and intelligence that surfs right past the rational
mind and into one's system to hang out acting all innocent in
the parking lot while secretly it's circulating, handing off associations, setting in motion all kinds of time-released, trouble-
making lexical disturbances, cognitive dissonance, which makes
my brain light up. Pussy Riot is up to no good in the best way,
practicing sacred art as a generative form of resistance, part of
a long lineage of performative disruptions which Alejandro
Jodorowski calls "psychomagic," because it's about soul, and it
starts with your name.
    Pussy Riot, as an entity, as individuals, as a revolutionary
movement motivated by dedication to nonviolent resistance
through creative acts of sacredness and interdependence of all
life, the thrilling quest of engaging with its mysteries, and the

innate right of everyone to develop their creativity and explore the nature of consciousness—you represent life and truth and most threateningly to the state, the power of heart combined with imagination and wit, against which no weapons are effective for long. Humor is always a giveaway of flexible intelligence, intact critical thinking skills, and worse yet, creativity and imagination. Virtually nothing enrages and terrifies authoritarian power more than irreverence and playfulness. Psychopathic rulers are cunning and ingenious when it comes to dominance and torture, but intellectually limited and humorless; their chief characteristic is paranoia and of course cowardice, and nothing frightens them more than unpredictability and loss of control, especially over language, the chief weapon of control.

Repressive brute power has the same game plan, always, and in this case the ubiquity of their surveillance and cold technology are diabolical and frightening. The magnetic field of the heart, though, is so powerful that science can't measure how far it extends, and it passes through anything the way neutrinos from space pass straight through the planet in a nanosecond. The gray metal jaws of the state apparatus that have slammed shut on you might as well be air. Which I say in terms of your ideas, because you yourself are being tortured physically and emotionally by cowering bullies. There are myriad channels of communication connecting all beings, though we're supposed to laugh at this notion. But science in its clunky way has proven repeatedly, for example, the power of prayer to heal instantaneously over great distances. Hearts in proximity to one another begin to synchronize within minutes. Thoughts travel faster than the speed of light. The universe, we are told, arises from the fabric of consciousness and it seems to be driven by creativity, playfulness, and a delight in beauty and the unexpected.

The entire ensouled universe is responding to your communications and magnifying them a zillion times. Maybe it was waiting for the spark of your ideas, a true magic, I think, the casting of a spell with impeccable intention. Your forty-second performance and statements during its aftermath are a stunningly articulate and concise description of our predicament and the possibilities for healing and transforming this terrible disease of psychopathy and malign death-infatuation, which has itself ensorcelled us into a sense of hopelessness. But there are levels of reality we can intuit though not see or fathom with our crude five senses, which I'm convinced you've activated globally. No brute physical force devised by primitive entities who vibrate at the level of thick tar from an oil spill and masquerade as authorities can stop the exponential dissemination of your ideas and actions outside the confines of time and space, far beyond even what the media has so helpfully supplied.

All of life exists currently under economic house arrest. We are inmates in a global prison, raped and pillaged on every level by a project of social engineering based on a sense of constant endangerment—economic, physical, intellectual—isolated from each other and the world in minds robbed of access to soul, transformed into prisons by terrorization through language, scapegoating, punishment of difference/creativity backed up by brute, random forms and eruptions of torture, and generalized pervasive fear. We are reduced to seeking the most basic necessities of life, and some creature comforts. Masha's descriptions of Russian orphans in psychiatric institutions, and the population in general, as benumbed, apathetic, intentionally deprived of access to education, devoid of imagination or even any connection to life itself, sounds exactly like the world I live in.

I share Masha's incomprehension that thousands of people are necessary to overthrow the handful of psychopaths who seem dedicated to turning the earth into a lifeless piece of charcoal. Why? Because they can. So powerful is the compulsion to dominate and destroy, even if it means they themselves are in a bunker somewhere, surrounded by smoking ruins, ruling over nothing but a hellscape of corpses or shuffling zombies . . . Where is the thrill in that?

And so, Pussy Riot, with your arrest, the state's mobilization of its vast media apparatus to defame you means that the term Pussy Riot is uttered incessantly by thousands, maybe millions of people, globally, each time detonating a host of linguistic associations, conscious or not, constellated around images—pussy, riot—that in this juxtaposition are shot through with compound and contradictory elements that simply will not yield interpretive closure or resolution, meaning that whoever utters or hears the term is activated to engage with the nature of language in general and this term in particular, repeatedly, like it or not.

Laurie Weeks *is the author of the award-winning novel* Zipper Mouth.

We Are Pussy Riot

Karen Finley

The Virgin Mary is Pussy Riot
Her annunciation
Her hot pussy bore the son of goddess

Eve the first woman is so Pussy Riot
Taking that first bite of apple
Leaving the Garden of Eden to a snake

Cleopatra is Pussy Riot in her Pussing Boots
Down the Nile to meet Antony
Claiming the throne as her own

Joan of Arc is hearing voices
Fighting for dear France and the good old
C'est la vie
Sounds like Pussy to me

Elizabeth I the Virgin Queen
Purring with my pussy
Riot Riot Riot

Mary Magdalene don't forget her
Her body is hers and ours
Pussy Riot touch me

Frida Kahlo
Her audacious creativity
Without the use of tweezers
God Bless

Gertrude Stein
A pussy is a pussy is a riot
Is a pussy a pussy riot puss

Josephine Baker is Pussy Riot
A la banana dance in Paris
How dare she!!

Virginia Woolf is writing it all down
Telling us like it is or isn't
Sometimes Pussy Riot is like that

Anna May Wong is surely Pussy Riot
Going against type for the full screen
Sojourner Truth is Pussy Riot
The underground railroad, an abolitionist
Moving us forward, setting the course

Georgia O'Keeffe painted pussy
Like no other
Our petals and undulations
Our spirit we possess
Our very pussy nature

Take me Pussy
Make me Pussy
I am Pussy Riot
We are all Pussy Riot now
FREE PUSSY RIOT

Karen Finley is an internationally acclaimed artist and writer whose work has been shown in museums and galleries around the world. She is the author of several books including A Different Kind of Intimacy, Shock Treatment, *and* The Reality Shows *and is currently a professor at the Tisch School of Art and Public Policy at NYU.*

The Feminist Press is an independent nonprofit literary publisher that promotes freedom of expression and social justice. We publish exciting authors who share an activist spirit and a belief in choice and equality. Founded in 1970, we began by rescuing "lost" works by writers such as Zora Neale Hurston and Charlotte Perkins Gilman, and established our publishing program with books by American writers of diverse racial and class backgrounds. Since then we have also been bringing works from around the world to North American readers. We seek out innovative, often surprising books that tell a different story.

See our complete list of books at **feministpress.org**, and join the Friends of FP to receive all our books at a great discount.

THE FEMINIST PRESS
AT THE CITY UNIVERSITY OF NEW YORK
FEMINISTPRESS.ORG